Business F724 / V705

TABLE OF CONTENTS
& ACKNOWLEDGEMENTS

PAGE

VENTURE CAPITAL AND PRIVATE EQUITY

Course Notes

Version 0.20130818

1

Chapter 1

AN INTRODUCTION TO PRIVATE EQUITY

Private investments are the most basic form of investments. All small businesses in North America are primarily structured as private companies, and as such, they form the very fabric of North American business. A very simple form of private investment is when you invest in your own business which is not traded on a stock exchange.

A **private company** is a company whose shares are not listed on a public stock market. An example of a public stock market is the New York Stock Exchange or the Toronto stock Exchange. Note that a private company may still have its bonds listed on a public stock market, but this bond listing does not make the company a public company. Facebook is an example of a company that was a private company but became public when it listed its shares on NASDAQ in 2012. Before the listing, the company was a private company and its investors were private investors.

While a great deal of information is available for public companies, most private companies exist in the realm of 'privacy'. The information available on private companies is usually sparse and is not subject to any systematic disclosure requirements. This feature of private companies makes it critical to obtain the necessary information using own research and due diligence. Several databases are available for further research including Capital IQ, Bloomberg, Thomson Reuters, and others.

WHAT IS PRIVATE EQUITY?

Private equity can be defined as the investment class for investment in private companies. It comes in a variety of flavors such as early-stage, later-stage, and growth-stage ventures. Leveraged buyouts and distressed debt investments also fall under the umbrella of private equity.

While private equity is considered the general private investment class, we will focus on two of its subclasses in these notes. We will combine the early, later, and growth stage investments into **venture capital**, which will contrast with the **leveraged buyouts** where the investment is made in mature stages in conjunction with unusually high levels of debt.

PRIVATE EQUITY FUND

A **private equity fund** is usually structured as an investment partnership or an investment trust although other structures are also possible. Let us consider the details of an investment partnership.

An investment partnership has two kinds of partners. A **limited partner** is usually the investor who is providing the capital to the fund to invest and is normally not involved in the operations of the fund. The liability of a limited partner is, as the name implies, limited to the capital invested by the partner. A **general partner**, on the other hand, is selected to run the operations of the fund including making decisions to invest in private companies, hiring personnel and service providers, doing the necessary research, and complying with the regulatory and financial reporting standards.

For example, institutional investors such as pension funds invest in Blackstone's private equity funds as limited partners. The managing partners and the supporting staff of Blackstone's investment firm are recruited by Blackstone's general partnership, which initially may not have any stake in the fund but may earn interest or fees over time with services provided and/or performance. Most of the limited partners are external investors such as pension funds; however, Blackstone's general partners may also invest in the fund as limited partners. This co-investment arrangement may be viewed favorably by other limited partners, as it would align the interests of the general partners with those of the limited partners.

Basic Private Equity Fund Structure — Diagram A

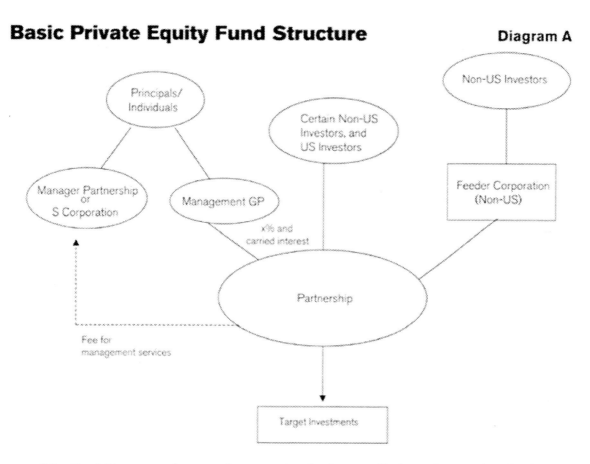

Because of the liquidity constraints, a private equity fund generally has a longer time horizon than public-market funds. Most private equity funds have an investment horizon of 5 to 7 years; a venture capital fund that focuses on early-stage investments may have a horizon as long as 10 years or more. This does not, however, mean that all investments of the fund last as long as the investment horizon. Instead, the sale of the last investment is completed by the end of the investment horizon of fund.

Given the investment horizons, the limited partners must also hold a long-term view of their investments. It should come as no surprise then that the typical investors in a private equity fund (that is, the limited partners) are institutional investors such as pension funds, insurance companies, endowments, and so on.

FUND ECONOMICS

The limited partners require a certain rate of return for investing in the fund. This required rate of return is a function of the risk of investing in the fund as evidenced by factors such as the liquidity of the fund, the riskiness of the underlying investments, longer-term time horizon, and a lack of available disclosures. Historically, the asset class has provided the following range of returns (based on NVCA's Benchmark Report as of December 2011).

U.S. VENTURE CAPITAL
Fund Index Summary
End-to-End Pooled Return, Net to Limited Partners
As of December 31, 2011

Index	1-Quarter	1-Year	3-Year	5-Year	10-Year	15-Year	20-Year	25-Year
Cambridge Associates LLC U.S. Venture Capital Index® [1]	**1.44**	**13.18**	**10.00**	**5.29**	**3.27**	**27.95**	**26.00**	**18.61**
U.S. Venture Capital - Early Stage Index [1]	**0.44**	**12.89**	**9.49**	**4.90**	**1.68**	**44.40**	**31.64**	**21.41**
U.S. Venture Capital - Late & Expansion Stage Index [1]	**3.05**	**15.15**	**17.99**	**10.52**	**7.56**	**12.55**	**19.88**	**15.64**
U.S. Venture Capital - Multi-Stage Index [1]	**2.36**	**12.87**	**7.84**	**3.81**	**4.71**	**17.15**	**20.06**	**15.45**
Barclays Capital Gov't/Credit Bond Index	1.18	8.74	6.60	6.55	5.85	6.36	6.56	7.16
Dow Jones Industrials Average	12.78	8.38	14.89	2.37	4.56	6.70	9.51	10.57
Dow Jones U.S. Small Cap Index	14.13	(3.17)	19.34	2.04	7.02	7.91	9.96	NA
Dow Jones U.S. TopCap Index	17.21	6.58	16.53	1.09	3.79	5.90	8.04	NA
Nasdaq Composite*	7.86	(1.80)	18.21	1.52	2.94	4.79	7.74	8.37
Russell 1000®	11.84	1.50	14.81	(0.02)	3.34	5.68	7.99	9.35
Russell 2000®	15.47	(4.18)	15.63	0.15	5.62	6.25	8.52	8.68
S&P 500	11.82	2.11	14.11	(0.25)	2.92	5.45	7.81	9.28
Wilshire 5000 Total Market	12.04	0.98	14.93	0.12	3.80	5.73	7.96	9.22

It is important to note that the returns are as observed by the limited partners. That is, the returns have been calculated after accounting for the fees charged by the general partner.

A typical private equity fund charges two types of fees (although other fees are not uncommon). At the very basic level, the fund charges a **management fee** which is calculated as a percentage of the higher of the total committed capital and the most recent valuation of net assets in the fund. For example, if the total capital committed is $100 MM, a management fee of 2% means that $2 MM will be charged by the general partner on an annual basis. Usually, the fee is payable on a monthly basis and is levied on the committed capital regardless of when the actual capital is provided to the fund.

Once capital has been committed, the limited partners are contractually bound to advance the funds as and when requested by the general partner. Usually, the general partner will request funds when a new investment has to be made. However, to provide for the management fees, the general partner will request more funds upfront. This management fee is used to pay the operating expenses of the fund such as salaries of the employees, expenses for service providers, technology and research expenses, financial reporting expenses, and so on.

It is important to realize that the funds provided by the limited partners must also be used to pay the management fee. For a $100-MM fund, if the annual management fee is $2 MM and the fund is expected to take 7 years to complete its investments, as much as $14 MM may be set aside to pay the management fee in the future. Assuming no or little interest earned on the management fee funds, only $86 MM of the committed capital is available for investment purposes.

While the management fees will keep the fund in business, a much bigger source of compensation for the general partner is the profits generated on the investments. In most cases, a private equity fund is also entitled to what we call a **performance fee**. This fee is charged on the profits generated on the investments. Typically, these fees will be 20% of the profits such that if the fund doubles from its initial capital of $100 MM, the profits of $100 MM will be shared 80% with the limited partners and 20% with the general partner. The performance fee, however, cannot be charged until the funds are returned to the limited partners and, as such, are mostly applicable after all investments have been sold and the fund is ready to be liquidated. The performance fee is also known as the **carried interest**. The fee structure of 2% management fee and 20% performance fee is also known as a 2/20 fee structure.

As can be seen from the discussion above, the general partner is compensated with the management and performance fees over the life of the fund. The limited partners are usually not on the hook for any more fees; however, in certain structures, additional fees may be charged for making an unusual investment or for providing a co-investment opportunity to the limited partners. In a co-investment opportunity, the limited partners invest directly in the investment alongside the fund. That is, while the fund is making an investment on their behalf, the limited partners can also make an additional investment directly into the company and not be subject to any management or performance fees on that additional investment.

Because of the fees charged by the general partner, the required returns on the underlying investments must be greater than the returns required by the limited partners on their investment into the fund. Most private equity funds do not revalue their investments in a company until the eventual sale. However, in certain cases, such as when doing a follow-up investment in a company already in the portfolio, revaluation at the time of the reinvestment may be necessary. The revaluation affects the calculation of the management fee in the subsequent months.

TAXATION

Funds structured as partnerships are not taxable entities, and the income or loss generated in the fund is flown through to the limited partners. Examples of income include capital gains, interest, and dividends.

Fees earned by the general partner are accrued as income to the general partner. If the general partner is structured as a partnership, then the income earned, classified as business income, is flown through to the partners, which may be individuals such as the managing partners of the general partnership. The general 'partnership' may also be a corporation which is then taxed on the income earned as it would be taxed on any business income.

PROBLEM 1.1

DGI Private Fund III is the third private equity fund raised by DGI and Co, a private equity firm located in Chicago. The limited partners have committed $100 MM under a 2/20 fee structure. Assume that the entire committed capital is requested by DGI and Co at the outset and that the fund has a five-year investment horizon which is when all investments will be liquidated and the resulting proceeds minus the fees will be returned to the Limited partners. Assume that no interest will be earned on any cash balance kept in the fund. No investment of the fund is revalued prior to the investment's exit.

Assuming that the annualized returns required by the limited partners on the investment in the fund are 20%, calculate the annualized returns that must be required by the general partner on the underlying investments.

Calculate the fees paid to the general partner on a year-by-year basis.

PROBLEM 1.2

ABR Investment Fund II is the second venture capital fund raised by ABR and Co, a venture capital firm located in San Francisco. The funds committed by the limited partners are $100 MM under a 2/20 fee structure.

The fund has a 10-year investment horizon. The present value of the entire stream of future management fees is drawn down by the general partner at the outset. The first investment will be made at the end of the first year for $40 MM. The second investment will be made at the end of the 2nd year for $25 MM. The third and the last investment will be made at the end of the 3rd year for the remaining committed capital.

The first investment will be exited at the end of the 8th year. The second investment will be exited at the end of the 9th year. The last investment will be exited at the end of the 10th year. After the last exit, the fund will be liquidated and the available cash minus the fees will be returned to the limited partners. The cash balance kept in the fund will accrue interest at 1%. No investment of the fund is revalued prior to the investment's exit.

Assuming that the annualized returns required by the general partner on the underlying investments is 25%, calculate the annualized returns observed by the limited partners on their investment in the fund.

PROBLEM 1.3

Provided below are the investments and the corresponding exits completed by a venture capital fund over its life. The fund returned all cash minus the fees to the limited partners at the end of the 8th year. The fund has a 2/20 fee structure, and any cash balance in the fund accrues interest at 1% per year. The management fee is charged on the higher of the amount of the committed capital and the most recent valuation of net assets in the fund.

Year 0: $80 MM committed, of which $6 MM is drawn down for the management fees
Year 1: $35 MM drawn down and invested in Company A
Year 2: $22 MM drawn down and invested in Company B
Year 3: Amount for the remaining management fees drawn down
Year 4: Remaining commitment drawn down and invested in Company C
Year 5: Company A sold for $112 MM and the cash proceeds kept in the fund
Year 6: Company B investment revalued to $40 MM
Year 7: Company B sold for $55 MM and the cash proceeds kept in the fund
Year 8: Company C investment written down to nil, the fund liquidated, and the cash balance minus the fees is returned to the limited partners

Calculate the annualized return (IRR) to the limited partners of the fund.

Chapter 2

FINANCIAL INSTRUMENTS IN PRIVATE EQUITY

A **financial instrument** is a tradable asset of any kind, such as cash or evidence of an ownership interest in an entity. A contractual right to receive, or deliver, cash or another financial instrument is also a financial instrument.

We will discuss several financial instruments in detail in this chapter as they apply to the private investments.

COMMON SHARES

Common shares (also known as **common stock**, **voting shares**, or **ordinary shares**) are a security that represents an ownership interest in a corporation. Common shares are normally the lowest ranking security in a corporation – that is, all other security holders must be repaid what is owed to them before common shareholders can receive any funds from the corporation. Note that only a corporation can have common shares; the equivalent securities for a partnership and a trust are the partnership units and the trust units respectively.

Common shares are termed "common" to distinguish them from preferred shares. If both types of shares exist, common shareholders cannot receive any funds from the corporation until all funds accrued to the preferred shareholders have been paid in full. Similarly, in the event of bankruptcy, common shareholders receive any remaining funds after bondholders, creditors, and preferred shareholders have been paid. If no such funds are remaining, the common shareholders will not receive anything.

The lack of **seniority** is well compensated with the upside potential. While the funds payable to other security holders are fixed or contractually defined, no such limitation exists for common shareholders. Common shareholders, thus, can theoretically receive an infinite amount of funds as long as the corporation has those funds available (today or in the future) and other security holders are paid what they have been owed. As the value of the corporation grows, the value of the common shares grows as well – usually at a faster rate.

Common shareholders normally also carry the right to vote on certain matters, such as electing the board of directors. As the board of directors recruit the top management of the corporation, the right to vote gives the common shareholders the effective control of the corporation proportional to the percentage of common shares owned. For example, if you own 40% of the voting common shares of a corporation, you own 40% of the voting rights. Normally, an ownership stake of more than 50% is considered a controlling stake – though other factors may also decide who has the effective control of the corporation.

Common shares can have multiple **classes** – such as Class A, Class B, and so on. The classes are usually created to redirect voting control among shareholders. As an example, in 2012, Facebook had two classes of common shares. The holder of Class A common shares were given more votes per common share than their Class B counterparts. Consequently, ownership of an equivalent number of common shares in Class B did not necessarily mean having the same voting power as that in Class A. As an extreme, a corporation can have both a "voting" and "non-voting" class of common shares. North American laws require the existence of at least one class of voting common shares.

Common shares are a perpetual security – that is, they do not have a maturity date. Common shareholders can receive funds from the corporation in one of the three ways:

1. Receive a dividend declared by the board of directors;
2. Have the company buy back or redeem the shares for their current market value (or agreed-upon value); and/or
3. Sell their shares to a third party for their current market value (or agreed-upon value).

The current market value of the common shareholders' aggregate claims on the corporation's assets is known as the **market value of equity** or the **market capitalization** or, simply, the **market cap**. The formulas are as follows:

Basic market cap = price per common share x number of common shares outstanding

Fully diluted market cap = price per common share x number of fully diluted common shares

The number of common shares outstanding is easy to determine by counting the number of shares listed as outstanding in the common share register. The corporation's quarterly and annual financial statements also provide this information.

The **fully diluted** common shares are the total number of common shares that would be outstanding if all other security holders who had a right to convert their securities (in part or in full) into common shares exercised their conversion rights. Under IFRS and US GAAP, in its financial statements, a corporation is required to report the fully diluted number of common shares resulting from conversion of all securities where the conversion will make the financial statements more conservative (i.e. benefit the converting shareholders at the expense of the existing shareholders).

Examples of securities that can be converted (in part or in full) into common shares include stock options, convertible bonds, warrants, rights, convertible preferred shares, and so on.

Unless otherwise noted, we will use the fully diluted definition of market cap in the remainder of these notes.

PREFERRED SHARES

Preferred shares (also known as **preferred stock, preference shares**, or, simply, **preferreds**) are a security with elements of both debt and equity. Preferred shares rank higher than the common shares but normally lower than other claimholders such as the bank, bondholders, and other creditors.

Ordinary preferred shares usually do not carry any voting rights, but they are entitled to a dividend and have priority over common shares in the payment of funds such as dividends and liquidation proceeds. Their liquidation value is contractually fixed – usually, at a value close to their face value.

Certain types of preferred shares, however, can have voting rights and the upside potential of the common shares.

FEATURES OF PREFERRED SHARES

Preferred shares are a special security which may have any combination of features not possessed by common shares, such as:

- Preference in dividends to common shareholders
- Preference in liquidating proceeds to common shareholders
- Ability to convert preferred shares into common shares
- Obligation to sell the shares back to the corporation at a predetermined price at the corporation's discretion
- Inability to vote

Ordinary preferred shares, sometimes referred to as the **plain-vanilla preferred shares**, act very much like a debt security but without any defined maturity. Such preferred shares are much like perpetual debt with the dividend replacing the coupon interest. The preferred shares will normally rank lower than other debt and, thus, carry a higher risk, a lower credit rating, and a higher yield. In contrast, while a fixed-maturity bond's market value approaches its par value as the maturity date nears, the perpetual nature of preferred shares makes them more susceptible to interest rate changes. Normally, preferred dividends, like common dividends, are not tax deductible for the corporation.

EXAMPLE OF PREFERRED SHARES

Listed on New York Stock Exchange in 2012 are the FPL Group Inc 5 7/8% Preferreds. This security tells us that the preferred shares are issued by FPL Group Inc (a corporation) and that they carry a dividend rate of 5.875% per annum. The face value of the shares in late July 2012 was $300 MM, but the required yield on the preferred shares fell below the dividend rate, thus, increasing the market value of the aggregate shares to $318 MM.

TYPES OF PREFERRED SHARES

Preferred shares are not commonplace among the publicly listed companies. Instead, the security is used extensively in private companies, where there is a need for separating the economics of securities based on the individual contributions and the associated risks.

The following are various flavors of the preferred shares.

Cumulative Preferred Shares

Preferred shares may be cumulative or noncumulative. A **cumulative preferred share** requires that if a corporation fails to pay a dividend below the stated rate, it must make up for the difference before any funds are payable to the common shareholders. Dividends accumulate with each quarter, semi-annual period, or year (as the case may be). A preferred share without this feature is known as a noncumulative preferred share; any dividends not declared are lost – suggesting a more 'common share' nature of the security.

In the FPL Group Inc's example above, suppose the company only pays a $15 MM aggregate dividend to its preferred shareholders in 2013. If the shares are cumulative, then the company still has to pay 5.875% * $300 MM - $15 MM = $2.625 MM to the preferred shareholders at a future date before any funds can be distributed to the common shareholders.

Convertible Preferred Shares

Much like a convertible bond, a **convertible preferred share** can be exchanged for a predetermined number of the corporation's common shares. This exchange may occur at any time the preferred shareholder chooses, regardless of the market price of the common stock, although a waiting or a vesting period may be involved.

After the exchange, the new common shares cannot be converted back into preferred shares. Logically, a preferred shareholder will convert into common shares only if the market value of the converted common shares exceeds the market value of the preferred shares.

For example, suppose you own 1,500 preferred shares that have a current market value of $10 per share (perhaps based on the fair value of those preferred shares) and can be converted into one common share each. As long as the common share price is below $10, you will keep your preferred share. If the price goes above $10, you will convert.

Participating Preferred Shares

Participating preferred shares are preferred shares that participate in the value of the company like common shares once the preferred part of their claims has been met. Like common shares, participating preferred shares represent partial interest in the company. Normally, the participating preferred shares are also cumulative.

In synthetic terms, a participating preferred share is a combination of a cumulative preferred share and a common stock.

Let us understand the concept by way of an example. Assume that a company has 10 participating preferred shares and 10 common shares outstanding. Each preferred share has a face value of $100. Ignore any dividends.

If the company is worth $800 in total, the participating preferred shares will be entitled to the entire $800 value of the company because $10 * 100 = $1,000 of the preferred claim is more than $800.

If the company is worth $1,000 in total, the participating preferred shares are still entitled to the entire $1,000 value of the company because $10 * 100 = $1,000 of the preferred claim equals $1,000.

If the company is worth $1,500 in total, the participating preferred shares will first receive their $1,000 face value, leaving $500 to be shared with the common shareholders. In total, 20 shares are outstanding (10 common and 10 preferred), which will share the $500 at a price of $500 / 20 = $2.5 per share. Participating preferred shareholders will, thus, receive $1,000 + 10 * $2.50 = $1,250, while the common shareholders will receive 10 * $2.50 = $250.

In other words, if $P_{PP\%,F,L}$ represents the proceeds to the participating preferred shares with a participation percentage of PP% and face value of F, then:

$$P_{PP\%,F} = \begin{cases} V_E & \text{if } V_E \leq F \\ F + PP\% * (V_E - F) & \text{if } V_E > F \end{cases}$$

Where V_E = value of the company's total equity (i.e. after paying down any debt)

Participating Preferred Shares with a Cap

As the name implies, a **participating** preferred share **with a cap** is a participating preferred share with a maximum limit on what the share can receive.

For example, assume that a company has 10 participating preferred shares and 10 common shares outstanding. Each preferred share has a face value of $100 and is capped at a value of three times the face value. Ignore any dividends.

If the company is worth $1,000 or less in total, the participating preferred shares will be entitled to the entire value of the company because $10 * 100 = $1,000 of the preferred claim is more than or equal to the value.

If the company is worth $1,500 in total, the participating preferred shares will first receive their $1,000 face value, leaving $500 to be shared with the common shareholders. In total, 20 shares are outstanding (10 common and 10 preferred), which will share the $500 at a price of $500 / 20 = $2.5 per share. Participating preferred shareholders will, thus, receive $1,000 + 10 * $2.50 = $1,250, while the common shareholders will receive 10 * $2.50 = $250.

If the company is worth $6,000 in total, then the participating preferred shares will first receive their $1,000 face value, leaving $5,000 to be shared with the common shareholders. Of the $5,000, once the first $4,000 has been shared 50-50 with the common shareholders, the participating preferred shareholders will have received $1,000 + $2,000 = $3,000 in total, which is equal to the cap of three times the aggregate face value of $1,000. Thus, the last $1,000 will go exclusively to the common shareholders.

In other words, if $P_{PP\%,F,L}$ represents the proceeds to the participating preferred shares with a participation percentage of PP%, face value of F, and a limit (or a cap) of L, then:

$$P_{PP\%,F,L} = \begin{cases} V_E & \text{if } V_E \leq F \\ F + PP\% * (V_E - F) & \text{if } F < V_E < F + (L - F) * PP\% \\ L & \text{if } V_E \geq F + (L - F) * PP\% \end{cases}$$

Where V_E = value of the company's total equity (i.e. after paying down any debt)

PREFERRED SHARE APPLICATIONS

Preferred shares are a flexible form of financing for a company. Given the flavors they come in, preferred shares can take on practically any given financing situation, with a focus on addressing the relative preferences and participation needs of different investors. Additionally, in contrast with debt, a company can normally defer a dividend with little penalty or little risk to its credit rating in the face of cash flow issues. Creative applications of the uses of preferred shares include prevention of hostile takeovers by associating extreme features to the preferred shares which are invoked only in the case of a hostile takeover.

A company, especially a small or young company, may issue preferred (and other) shares in multiple rounds of financing. For example, Twitter's 'Series A' round of funding was for an amount rumored to have been between $1 MM and $5 MM. The 'Series B' round of funding in 2008 was for $22 MM, while the 'Series C' round of funding in 2009 was for $35 MM from Institutional Venture Partners, Benchmark Capital, and others. The term 'series' is used to define the **vintage** of the financing issue – that is, the financing round in which the shares were issued. Typically, investments made in subsequent rounds rank higher in preference than those in the previous rounds.

Convertible preferred shares and participating preferred shares (with or without the cap) are extensively used by private equity firm, especially the venture capital firms. That is, instead of receiving common shares for their investment in a company, the venture capital firm receives, say, participating preferred shares. The venture capital firms are bringing in the capital or the money, so the convertible or participating preferred shares provide their shares some level of preference over those of the entrepreneurs.

The use of preferred shares in such disparate settings is not universal, however. One alternative solution may be to issue common shares to the investors and only stock options to the entrepreneurs. Another alternative may be to issue common shares to all parties and also issue warrants to the investors. In any case, the distinction between the securities held by the investors and those held by the entrepreneurs is an important one. The equity earned or monetized by the entrepreneur by increasing the value of the company is known as the **sweat equity**.

Convertible or participating preferred shares are often used as a "bridge" between a company that desires a higher valuation and an investor that believes in a lower valuation. The investor can agree to a higher valuation if it is accompanied by a participating preferred security, essentially challenging the company to earn the upside of the higher valuation. At the end of the day, any feature associated with the preferred shares is a result of the negotiations between the parties.

VENTURE DEBT

Most early-stage or small businesses usually do not qualify to take on debt from traditional sources such as a bank. The reality is that the cash flows of small business are uncertain and, in the case of an early-stage company, overwhelmingly negative. Most debt arrangements require periodic repayment of interest and, occasionally, the principal.

Nevertheless, specialized lenders can still fund working capital and capital expenditures by using a form of debt known as the **venture debt**. In such cases, no interest payment is due periodically (at least for an initial period of time), and the debt financing is structured primarily as a zero-coupon debt. The lender is usually looking for collateral such as an equipment or accounts receivable.

To entice lenders to provide venture debt to early-stage, high-risk companies, the debt issue also provides free warrants or stock options to the lender. As a result, venture debt is really a combination of debt and equity, with the equity represented by an option. Convertible debt is a formal way of creating this hybrid relationship, and all venture debt ranks higher in preference to the preferred and common shares.

Loan terms are wide ranging. Repayment time horizon is 12 to 48 months, and the required yield to maturity is typically between 12% and 20%. Almost 100% of an equipment purchase can be financed but usually only about 80% of current assets such as inventory and accounts receivable. The fair market value of warrants or options at the time of the grant will normally be in the range of 10% to 30% of the loan value.

TAXATION ISSUES

Any dividends paid on the equity securities are not deductible for tax purposes in North America by the company. Any interest expense paid on the debt securities, however, is. Hence, dividends paid on common shares are not deductible, while the interest paid (or accrued and then paid) on the venture debt is deductible.

Preferred dividends, although fixed like interest on debt, are paid out of the after-tax earnings of a company and are deducted from the retained earnings. As such, preferred dividends are still considered dividends and are not deductible for tax purposes in North America – unless it can be shown, for example, that the dividends have to be mandatorily paid like contractual interest or the preferred shares must be redeemed mandatorily at some point in the future.

On July 30, 2012, Wal-Mart has 3.38 billion common shares outstanding and 3.51 billion fully diluted common shares. Assuming a stock price of $75, calculate the basic and fully diluted market cap of the company.

Franktill Corporation has 2 MM shares outstanding and 2 MM warrants outstanding with each warrant giving the holder a right to buy one common share at a price of $4 per share. If the current price is $5 per share, calculate the basic and fully diluted market cap of the company.

A company is worth $200 MM today. The capital structure, in the order of preference, is as follows:

- 50,000 Series B preferred shares, participating, face value of $1,000 per share
- 30,000 Series A preferred shares, participating, face value of $500 per share
- 100,000 common shares

If redeemed, the preferential proceeds to each category of shares will equal their face values. All declared dividends have already been paid. If the company is liquidated today, calculate the total proceeds to be received by each category of shares.

A company is worth $450 MM today. The capital structure, in the order of preference, is as follows:

- 50,000 Series C preferred shares, convertible into one common share each, face value of $1,000
- 40,000 Series B preferred shares, participating, face value of $1,000 per share
- 20,000 Series A preferred shares, participating, face value of $500 per share
- 90,000 common shares

If redeemed, the preferential proceeds to each category of shares will equal their face values. All declared dividends have already been paid. If the company is liquidated today, calculate the total proceeds to be received by each category of shares.

PROBLEM 2.5

A company is worth $600 MM today. The capital structure, in the order of preference, is as follows:

- 50,000 Series C preferred shares, convertible into one common share each, face value of $1,000 per share, 5% cumulative dividend rate, issued one year ago
- 50,000 Series B preferred shares, participating, face value of $800 per share, 6% cumulative dividend rate, issued two years ago
- 25,000 Series A preferred shares, participating, face value of $600 per share, 8% cumulative dividend rate, issued four years ago
- 90,000 common shares

If redeemed, the preferential proceeds to each category of shares will equal their face values plus any declared but unpaid dividends. No dividend has ever been paid in the company's history on any share. If the company is liquidated today, calculate the total proceeds to be received by each category of shares.

PROBLEM 2.6

A company is worth $500 MM today. The capital structure, in the order of preference, is as follows:

- Zero-coupon debt of $10 MM face value, currently yielding 5% to maturity (which is in two years' time)
- 50,000 Series B preferred shares, participating with a limit of three times the face value, face value of $1,000 per share, face value of $1,000, 6% cumulative dividend rate, issued two years ago
- 50,000 Series A preferred shares, participating, face value of $500 per share, 8% cumulative dividend rate, issued three years ago
- 100,000 common shares

Additionally, the venture debt has a total of 50,000 warrants associated with it, with each warrant giving the debt holder the right to purchase one common share at a price of $500 per share. The warrants can be exercised today.

If redeemed, the preferential proceeds to each category of shares will equal their face values plus any declared but unpaid dividends. No dividend has ever been paid in the company's history on any share. If the company is liquidated today, calculate the total proceeds to be received by each category of shares.

A company is worth $650 MM today. The capital structure, in the order of preference, is as follows:

- Zero-coupon debt of $20 MM face value, currently yielding 5% to maturity (which is in three years' time)
- 50,000 Series B preferred shares, participating with a limit of three times the face value, face value of $1,000 per share, 6% cumulative dividend rate, issued two years ago
- 40,000 Series A preferred shares, convertible into one common share each, face value of $1,000 per share, 8% cumulative dividend rate, issued four years ago
- 80,000 common shares

Additionally, the venture debt has a total of 100,000 warrants associated with it, with each warrant giving the debt holder the right to purchase one common share at a price of $400 per share. The warrants can be exercised today.

If redeemed, the preferential proceeds to each category of shares will equal their face values plus any declared but unpaid dividends. No dividend has ever been paid in the company's history on any share. If the company is liquidated today, calculate the total proceeds to be received by each category of shares.

Chapter 3

VENTURE CAPITAL TERM SHEETS

© Adeel Mahmood, 2012

A **term sheet** is a business document that outlines the major terms and conditions of an agreement or an arrangement. While it is not necessarily legally binding, it guides the detailed legal document that is subsequently drafted by the lawyers. A term sheet is, thus, considered a document that outlines the intended legal agreement that will become binding.

A term sheet that is signed by both parties, however, can have a legal basis – i.e. the terms agreed upon can be enforced. The exact binding nature of the terms depends upon the language used in the term sheet. In venture capital – and, generally, private equity – because of the reputational risk associated with walking away from such an agreement, most parties will not propose a term sheet unless either it has already been approved by the legal counsel or the terms included overwhelmingly favor the proposing party.

Once an initial term sheet has been presented, negotiations usually follow on the key terms that are important to either party. After several iterations, once a final term sheet emerges, it is signed and then sent over to the lawyers for conversion to a full legal document. As such, a term sheet on its own need not be very detailed – but, in many cases, it is.

In the pages that follow, we present a venture capital term sheet adapted from the version publicly available on the website of National Venture Capital Association (NVCA). The original term sheet used by NVCA attempts to cover most bases and may be unreasonably detailed for most agreements. We have modified it to focus on the terms that a venture capital deal is most likely to encounter. The full version is available from the course website.

The following disclaimer provided by NVCA is equally applicable to the modified term sheet.

This sample document is the work product of a national coalition of attorneys who specialize in venture capital financings, working under the auspices of the NVCA. This document is intended to serve as a starting point only, and should be tailored to meet your specific requirements. This document should not be construed as legal advice for any particular facts or circumstances. Note that this sample document presents an array of (often mutually exclusive) options with respect to particular deal provisions.

TERM SHEET
FOR SERIES A PREFERRED STOCK FINANCING OF
[INSERT COMPANY NAME], **INC.**
[_____ __, 20__]

This Term Sheet summarizes the principal terms of the Series A Preferred Stock Financing of [_____], Inc., a [Delaware] corporation (the "**Company**"). In consideration of the time and expense devoted and to be devoted by the Investors with respect to this investment, the No Shop/Confidentiality [and Counsel and Expenses] provisions of this Term Sheet shall be binding obligations of the Company whether or not the financing is consummated. No other legally binding obligations will be created until definitive agreements are executed and delivered by all parties. This Term Sheet is not a commitment to invest, and is conditioned on the completion of due diligence, legal review and documentation that is satisfactory to the Investors. This Term Sheet shall be governed in all respects by the laws of the [State of Delaware].

Offering Terms

Closing Date:	As soon as practicable following the Company's acceptance of this Term Sheet and satisfaction of the Conditions to Closing (the "**Closing**"). [*provide for multiple closings if applicable*]
Investors:	Investor No. 1: [_____] shares ([__]%), $[_____]
	Investor No. 2: [_____] shares ([__]%), $[_____]
	[as well other investors mutually agreed upon by Investors and the Company]
Amount Raised:	$[_____], [including $[_____] from the conversion of principal [and interest] on bridge notes].[1]
Price Per Share:	$[_____] per share (based on the capitalization of the Company set forth below) (the "**Original Purchase Price**").
Pre-Money Valuation:	The Original Purchase Price is based upon a fully-diluted pre-money valuation of $[_____] and a fully-diluted post-money valuation of $[_____] (including an employee pool representing [__]% of the fully-diluted post-money capitalization).
Capitalization:	The Company's capital structure before and after the Closing is set forth <u>on Exhibit A.</u>
Dividends:	[*Alternative 1:* Dividends will be paid on the Series A Preferred on an as-converted basis when, as, and if paid on the Common Stock]

---

[1] Modify this provision to account for staged investments or investments dependent on the achievement of milestones by the Company.

*[Alternative 2: The Series A Preferred will carry an annual [ ]%
cumulative dividend [payable upon a liquidation or redemption].
For any other dividends or distributions, participation with Common
Stock on an as-converted basis.]* [2]

[Alternative 3: Non-cumulative dividends will be paid on the Series
A Preferred in an amount equal to $[_____] per share of Series A
Preferred when and if declared by the Board.]

Liquidation Preference:

In the event of any liquidation, dissolution or winding up of the
Company, the proceeds shall be paid as follows:

[Alternative 1 (non-participating Preferred Stock): First pay [one]
times the Original Purchase Price [plus accrued dividends] [plus
declared and unpaid dividends] on each share of Series A Preferred.
The balance of any proceeds shall be distributed pro rata to holders
of Common Stock.]

[Alternative 2 (full participating Preferred Stock): First pay [one]
times the Original Purchase Price [plus accrued dividends] [plus
declared and unpaid dividends] on each share of Series A Preferred.
Thereafter, the Series A Preferred participates with the Common
Stock pro rata on an as-converted basis.]

[Alternative 3 (cap on Preferred Stock participation rights): First
pay [one] times the Original Purchase Price [plus accrued dividends]
[plus declared and unpaid dividends] on each share of Series A
Preferred. Thereafter, Series A Preferred participates with Common
Stock pro rata on an as-converted basis until the holders of Series A
Preferred receive an aggregate of [_____] times the Original
Purchase Price (including the amount paid pursuant to the preceding
sentence).]

A merger or consolidation (other than one in which stockholders of
the Company own a majority by voting power of the outstanding
shares of the surviving or acquiring corporation) and a sale, lease,
transfer, exclusive license or other disposition of all or substantially
all of the assets of the Company will be treated as a liquidation event
(a **"Deemed Liquidation Event"**), thereby triggering payment of
the liquidation preferences described above [unless the holders of
[___]% of the Series A Preferred elect otherwise]. [The Investors'
entitlement to their liquidation preference shall not be abrogated or
diminished in the event part of the consideration is subject to escrow

---

[2] In some cases, accrued and unpaid dividends are payable on conversion as well as upon a liquidation event.
Most typically, however, dividends are not paid if the preferred is converted. Another alternative is to give the
Company the option to pay accrued and unpaid dividends in cash or in common shares valued at fair market value. The
latter are referred to as "PIK" (payment-in-kind) dividends.

in connection with a Deemed Liquidation Event.][3]

Voting Rights:

The Series A Preferred shall vote together with the Common Stock on an as-converted basis, and not as a separate class, except (i) [so long as [*insert fixed number, or %, or "any"*] shares of Series A Preferred are outstanding,] the Series A Preferred as a class shall be entitled to elect [_____] [(_)] members of the Board (the "**Series A Directors**"), and (ii) as required by law. The Company's Certificate of Incorporation will provide that the number of authorized shares of Common Stock may be increased or decreased with the approval of a majority of the Preferred and Common Stock, voting together as a single class, and without a separate class vote by the Common Stock.[4]

Protective Provisions:

[So long as [*insert fixed number, or %, or "any"*] shares of Series A Preferred are outstanding,] in addition to any other vote or approval required under the Company's Charter or By-laws, the Company will not, without the written consent of the holders of at least [__]% of the Company's Series A Preferred, either directly or by amendment, merger, consolidation, or otherwise:

(i) liquidate, dissolve or wind-up the affairs of the Company, or effect any merger or consolidation or any other Deemed Liquidation Event; (ii) amend, alter, or repeal any provision of the Certificate of Incorporation or Bylaws [in a manner adverse to the Series A Preferred];[5] (iii) create or authorize the creation of or issue any other security convertible into or exercisable for any equity security, having rights, preferences or privileges senior to or on parity with the Series A Preferred, or increase the authorized number of shares of Series A Preferred; (iv) purchase or redeem or pay any dividend on any capital stock prior to the Series A Preferred, [other than stock repurchased from former employees or consultants in connection with the cessation of their employment/services, at the lower of fair market value or cost;] [other than as approved by the Board, including the approval of [____] Series A Director(s)]; or (v) create or authorize the creation of any debt security [if the Company's aggregate indebtedness would exceed $[____][other than

---

[3] See Subsection 2.3.4 of the Model Certificate of Incorporation and the detailed explanation in related footnote 25.

[4] For corporations incorporated in California, one cannot "opt out" of the statutory requirement of a separate class vote by Common Stockholders to authorize shares of Common Stock. The purpose of this provision is to "opt out" of DGL 242(b)(2).

[5] Note that as a matter of background law, Section 242(b)(2) of the Delaware General Corporation Law provides that if any proposed charter amendment would adversely alter the rights, preferences and powers of one series of Preferred Stock, but not similarly adversely alter the entire class of all Preferred Stock, then the holders of that series are entitled to a separate series vote on the amendment.

equipment leases or bank lines of credit][unless such debt security has received the prior approval of the Board of Directors, including the approval of [_____] Series A Director(s)]; (vi) create or hold capital stock in any subsidiary that is not a wholly-owned subsidiary or dispose of any subsidiary stock or all or substantially all of any subsidiary assets; [or (vii) increase or decrease the size of the Board of Directors].[6]

Optional Conversion:

The Series A Preferred initially converts 1:1 to Common Stock at any time at option of holder, subject to adjustments for stock dividends, splits, combinations and similar events and as described below under "Anti-dilution Provisions."

Anti-dilution Provisions:

In the event that the Company issues additional securities at a purchase price less than the current Series A Preferred conversion price, such conversion price shall be adjusted in accordance with the following formula:

[*Alternative 1:* "Typical" weighted average:

$$CP_2 = CP_1 * (A+B) / (A+C)$$

CP_2 = Series A Conversion Price in effect immediately after new issue

CP_1 = Series A Conversion Price in effect immediately prior to new issue

A = Number of shares of Common Stock deemed to be outstanding immediately prior to new issue (includes all shares of outstanding common stock, all shares of outstanding preferred stock on an as-converted basis, and all outstanding options on an as-exercised basis; and does not include any convertible securities converting into this round of financing)[7]

B = Aggregate consideration received by the Corporation with respect to the new issue divided by CP_1

C = Number of shares of stock issued in the subject transaction]

[*Alternative 2:* Full-ratchet – the conversion price will be reduced to the price at which the new shares are issued.]

[*Alternative 3*: No price-based anti-dilution protection.]

---

[6] The board size provision may also be addressed in the Voting Agreement; see Section 1.1 of the Model Voting Agreement.

[7] The "broadest" base would include shares reserved in the option pool.

The following issuances shall not trigger anti-dilution adjustment:[8]

(i) securities issuable upon conversion of any of the Series A Preferred, or as a dividend or distribution on the Series A Preferred; (ii) securities issued upon the conversion of any debenture, warrant, option, or other convertible security; (iii) Common Stock issuable upon a stock split, stock dividend, or any subdivision of shares of Common Stock; and (iv) shares of Common Stock (or options to purchase such shares of Common Stock) issued or issuable to employees or directors of, or consultants to, the Company pursuant to any plan approved by the Company's Board of Directors [including at least [_____] Series A Director(s)].

Mandatory Conversion: Each share of Series A Preferred will automatically be converted into Common Stock at the then applicable conversion rate in the event of the closing of a [firm commitment] underwritten public offering with a price of [___] times the Original Purchase Price (subject to adjustments for stock dividends, splits, combinations and similar events) and [net/gross] proceeds to the Company of not less than $[_____] (a "**QPO**"), or (ii) upon the written consent of the holders of [__]% of the Series A Preferred.[9]

[Pay-to-Play: [Unless the holders of [__]% of the Series A elect otherwise,] on any subsequent [down] round all [Major] Investors are required to purchase their pro rata share of the securities set aside by the Board for purchase by the [Major] Investors. All shares of Series A Preferred[10] of any [Major] Investor failing to do so will automatically [lose anti-dilution rights] [lose right to participate in future rounds] [convert to Common Stock and lose the right to a Board seat if applicable].[11]

---

[8] Note that additional exclusions are frequently negotiated, such as issuances in connection with equipment leasing and commercial borrowing. See Subsections 4.4.1(d)(v)-(viii) of the Model Certificate of Incorporation for additional exclusions.

[9] The per share test ensures that the investor achieves a significant return on investment before the Company can go public. Also consider allowing a non-QPO to become a QPO if an adjustment is made to the Conversion Price for the benefit of the investor, so that the investor does not have the power to block a public offering.

[10] Alternatively, this provision could apply on a proportionate basis (e.g., if Investor plays for ½ of pro rata share, receives ½ of anti-dilution adjustment).

[11] If the punishment for failure to participate is losing some but not all rights of the Preferred (e.g., anything other than a forced conversion to common), the Certificate of Incorporation will need to have so-called "blank check preferred" provisions at least to the extent necessary to enable the Board to issue a "shadow" class of preferred with diminished rights in the event an investor fails to participate. Because these provisions flow through the charter, an alternative Model Certificate of Incorporation with "pay-to-play lite" provisions (e.g., shadow Preferred) has been posted. As a drafting matter, it is far easier to simply have (some or all of) the preferred convert to common.

Redemption Rights:[12]	Unless prohibited by Delaware law governing distributions to stockholders, the Series A Preferred shall be redeemable at the option of holders of at least [__]% of the Series A Preferred commencing any time after [_____] at a price equal to the Original Purchase Price [plus all accrued but unpaid dividends]. Redemption shall occur in three equal annual portions. Upon a redemption request from the holders of the required percentage of the Series A Preferred, all Series A Preferred shares shall be redeemed [(except for any Series A holders who affirmatively opt-out)].[13]
Representations and Warranties:	Standard representations and warranties by the Company. [Representations and warranties by Founders regarding [technology ownership, etc.].[14]
Right to Participate Pro Rata in Future Rounds:	All [Major] Investors shall have a pro rata right, based on their percentage equity ownership in the Company (assuming the conversion of all outstanding Preferred Stock into Common Stock and the exercise of all options outstanding under the Company's stock plans), to participate in subsequent issuances of equity securities of the Company (excluding those issuances listed at the end of the "Anti-dilution Provisions" section of this Term Sheet. In addition, should any [Major] Investor choose not to purchase its full pro rata share, the remaining [Major] Investors shall have the right to purchase the remaining pro rata shares.
Matters Requiring Investor Director Approval:	[So long as the holders of Series A Preferred are entitled to elect a Series A Director, the Company will not, without Board approval, which approval must include the affirmative vote of [one/both] of

---

[12]   Redemption rights allow Investors to force the Company to redeem their shares at cost (and sometimes investors may also request a small guaranteed rate of return, in the form of a dividend). In practice, redemption rights are not often used; however, they do provide a form of exit and some possible leverage over the Company. While it is possible that the right to receive dividends on redemption could give rise to a Code Section 305 "deemed dividend" problem, many tax practitioners take the view that if the liquidation preference provisions in the Charter are drafted to provide that, on conversion, the holder receives the greater of its liquidation preference or its as-converted amount (as provided in the Model Certificate of Incorporation), then there is no Section 305 issue.

[13]   Due to statutory restrictions, the Company may not be legally permitted to redeem in the very circumstances where investors most want it (the so-called "sideways situation"). Accordingly, and particulary in light of the Delaware Chancery Court's ruling in *Thoughtworks (*see discussion in Model Charter*),* investors may seek enforcement provisions to give their redemption rights more teeth - - e.g., the redemption amount shall be paid in the form of a one-year note to each unredeemed holder of Series A Preferred, and the holders of a majority of the Series A Preferred shall be entitled to elect a majority of the Company's Board of Directors until such amounts are paid in full.

[14]   Founders' representations are controversial and may elicit significant resistance as they are found in a minority of venture deals. They are more likely to appear if Founders are receiving liquidity from the transaction, or if there is heightened concern over intellectual property (e.g., the Company is a spin-out from an academic institution or the Founder was formerly with another company whose business could be deemed competitive with the Company), or in international deals. Founders' representations are even less common in subsequent rounds, where risk is viewed as significantly diminished and fairly shared by the investors, rather than being disproportionately borne by the Founders. A sample set of Founders Representations is attached as an Addendum at the end of the Model Stock Purchase Agreement.

the Series A Director(s):

(i) make any loan or advance to, or own any stock or other securities of, any subsidiary or other corporation, partnership, or other entity unless it is wholly owned by the Company; (ii) make any loan or advance to any person, including, any employee or director, except advances and similar expenditures in the ordinary course of business or under the terms of a employee stock or option plan approved by the Board of Directors; (iii) guarantee, any indebtedness except for trade accounts of the Company or any subsidiary arising in the ordinary course of business; (iv) make any investment inconsistent with any investment policy approved by the Board; (v) incur any aggregate indebtedness in excess of $[____] that is not already included in a Board-approved budget, other than trade credit incurred in the ordinary course of business; (vi) enter into or be a party to any transaction with any director, officer or employee of the Company or any "associate" (as defined in Rule 12b-2 promulgated under the Exchange Act) of any such person [except transactions resulting in payments to or by the Company in an amount less than $[60,000] per year], [or transactions made in the ordinary course of business and pursuant to reasonable requirements of the Company's business and upon fair and reasonable terms that are approved by a majority of the Board of Directors];[15] (vii) hire, fire, or change the compensation of the executive officers, including approving any option grants; (viii) change the principal business of the Company, enter new lines of business, or exit the current line of business; (ix) sell, assign, license, pledge or encumber material technology or intellectual property, other than licenses granted in the ordinary course of business; or (x) enter into any corporate strategic relationship involving the payment contribution or assignment by the Company or to the Company of assets greater than [$100,000.00].

Non-Competition and Non-Solicitation Agreements:[16]

Each Founder and key employee will enter into a [one] year non-competition and non-solicitation agreement in a form reasonably

---

[15]   Note that Section 402 of the Sarbanes-Oxley Act of 2003 would require repayment of any loans in full prior to the Company filing a registration statement for an IPO.

[16]   Note that non-compete restrictions (other than in connection with the sale of a business) are prohibited in California, and may not be enforceable in other jurisdictions, as well. In addition, some investors do not require such agreements for fear that employees will request additional consideration in exchange for signing a Non-Compete/Non-Solicit (and indeed the agreement may arguably be invalid absent such additional consideration - - although having an employee sign a non-compete contemporaneous with hiring constitutes adequate consideration in jurisdictions where non-competes are generally enforceable). Others take the view that it should be up to the Board on a case-by-case basis to determine whether any particular key employee is required to sign such an agreement. Non-competes typically have a one year duration, although state law may permit up to two years.

acceptable to the Investors.

Employee Stock Options:

All employee options to vest as follows: [25% after one year, with remaining vesting monthly over next 36 months].

[Immediately prior to the Series A Preferred Stock investment, [_____] shares will be added to the option pool creating an unallocated option pool of [_____] shares.]

Right of first Refusal/
Right of Co-Sale (Take-me-Along):

Company first and Investors second (to the extent assigned by the Board of Directors,) will have a right of first refusal with respect to any shares of capital stock of the Company proposed to be transferred by Founders [and future employees holding greater than [1]% of Company Common Stock (assuming conversion of Preferred Stock and whether then held or subject to the exercise of options)], with a right of oversubscription for Investors of shares unsubscribed by the other Investors. Before any such person may sell Common Stock, he will give the Investors an opportunity to participate in such sale on a basis proportionate to the amount of securities held by the seller and those held by the participating Investors.[17]

Board of Directors:

At the initial Closing, the Board shall consist of [_____] members comprised of (i) [*Name*] as [the representative designated by [_____], as the lead Investor, (ii) [*Name*] as the representative designated by the remaining Investors, (iii) [*Name*] as the representative designated by the Founders, (iv) the person then serving as the Chief Executive Officer of the Company, and (v) [___] person(s) who are not employed by the Company and who are mutually acceptable [to the Founders and Investors][to the other directors].

[<u>DragAlong</u>:

Holders of Preferred Stock and the Founders [and all future holders of greater than [1]% of Common Stock (assuming conversion of Preferred Stock and whether then held or subject to the exercise of options)] shall be required to enter into an agreement with the Investors that provides that such stockholders will vote their shares in favor of a Deemed Liquidation Event or transaction in which 50% or more of the voting power of the Company is transferred and which is approved by [the Board of Directors] [and the holders of ____% of the outstanding shares of Preferred Stock, on an as-converted basis (the "**Electing Holders**")], so long as the liability of each stockholder in such transaction is several (and not joint) and does not exceed the stockholder's pro rata portion of any claim and the consideration to be paid to the stockholders in such transaction

---

[17]   Certain exceptions are typically negotiated, e.g., estate planning or *de minimis* transfers. Investors may also seek ROFR rights with respect to transfers by investors, in order to be able to have some control over the composition of the investor group.

will be allocated as if the consideration were the proceeds to be distributed to the Company's stockholders in a liquidation under the Company's then-current Certificate of Incorporation.][18]

Founders' Stock:	All Founders to own stock outright subject to Company right to buyback at cost. Buyback right for [__]% for first [12 months] after Closing; thereafter, right lapses in equal [monthly] increments over following [__] months.
No Shop/Confidentiality:	The Company agrees to work in good faith expeditiously towards a closing. The Company and the Founders agree that they will not, for a period of [_____] weeks from the date these terms are accepted, take any action to solicit, initiate, encourage or assist the submission of any proposal, negotiation or offer from any person or entity other than the Investors relating to the sale or issuance, of any of the capital stock of the Company [or the acquisition, sale, lease, license or other disposition of the Company or any material part of the stock or assets of the Company] and shall notify the Investors promptly of any inquiries by any third parties in regards to the foregoing. [In the event that the Company breaches this no-shop obligation and, prior to [_____], closes any of the above-referenced transactions [without providing the Investors the opportunity to invest on the same terms as the other parties to such transaction], then the Company shall pay to the Investors $[_____] upon the closing of any such transaction as liquidated damages.][19] The Company will not disclose the terms of this Term Sheet to any person other than officers, members of the Board of Directors and the Company's accountants and attorneys and other potential Investors acceptable to [_____], as lead Investor, without the written consent of the Investors.
Expiration:	This Term Sheet expires on [_____ __, 20__] if not accepted by the Company by that date.

EXECUTED THIS [__] DAY OF [_____],20[__].

[SIGNATURE BLOCKS]

---

[18]   See Subsection 3.3 of the Model Voting Agreement for a more detailed list o f conditions that must be satisfied in order for the drag-along to be invoked.

[19]   It is unusual to provide for such "break-up" fees in connection with a venture capital financing, but might be something to consider where there is a substantial possibility the Company may be sold prior to consummation of the financing (e.g., a later stage deal).

EXHIBIT A

Pre- and Post-Financing Capitalization

Security	Pre-Financing		Post-Financing	
	# of Shares	%	# of Shares	%
Common – Founders				
Common – Employee Stock Pool				
_____ Issued				
_____ Unissued				
[Common – Warrants]				
Series A Preferred				
Total				

34

The modified term sheet includes several terms, but we will focus our discussion on certain key terms that are typically more difficult to understand.

The **Closing Date** refers to the date on which the venture capital financing will be closed. The **Investors** section provides the names, shareholding percentages, and amounts invested of the new investors, including the venture capital firm. If there are multiple investors involved, these details may instead be listed in an appendix or exhibit and referred to in this section.

The **Amount Raised** is the total financing amount, and the **Price per Share** is the Amount Raised divided by the total number of shares being issued to the investors. The **Dividends** section outlines the details of the amount and nature of dividends, if any, payable on the shares. The concepts of **Pre-Money Valuation** and **Capitalization** will be discussed in a later chapter.

Liquidation Preference is discussed later in this chapter.

Voting Rights outline the nature of voting privileges for the investors based on their shareholdings. **Protective Provisions** prevent the company (which may be represented by the founders and/or the management team) from making major strategic decisions unilaterally. Examples of such decisions include liquidation or dissolution of the company, engagement in mergers and acquisitions, and so on. The provisions here require that a minimum percentage of the votes cast by the investors be in favor of such decisions.

Optional Conversion outlines the conversion rights of the investors – that is, their rights to convert their preferred shares into common shares. **Anti-dilution** Provisions are discussed later in this chapter.

Mandatory Conversion makes the investors (that is, the holders of the preferred shares) convert their shares into common shares automatically when a major liquidation or sale event (such as an IPO) takes place to the satisfaction of the investors. This provision ensures that a preferred shareholder not converting despite a satisfactory return on investment does not hinder the liquidation or sale process. Usually, a major liquidation or sale event takes place without any earlier news to that effect, and the buyers are not automatically keen on having preferred shareholders in the new capital structure.

The **Pay-to-Play** provisions essentially forces the investors to purchase the shares that they promised to purchase and give the company the promised funds in exchange for. **Redemptions Rights**, if present, allow the investors to force a sale of their shares back to the company for the indicated amounts – that is, redeem their shares. The **Representation and Warranties** are the standard representation and warranties in any business contract but may delay the signing of the term sheet as described in the footnotes to the term sheet provided.

The **Right to Participate Pro Rata in Future Rounds** allows the investors to preserve their shareholding percentage in the future financing rounds when new funds are raised. With the right, the investors can buy shares in the future rounds and not get diluted by new investors fully or partly.

The **Matters Requiring Investor Director Approval** tend to be the major corporate decisions that the investors would like to have their consent with. Usually, the investors' representative on the Board of Directors would keep this veto power, and the section here differs from the one on the Protective Provisions in that the terms here protect the investors from the adverse effects of the *internal* or *administrative* corporate decisions.

Non-Competition and Non-Solicitation Agreements are the standard agreements to prevent the founders and key employees from engaging after their own departure from the company in competition or solicitation of the remaining employees. The **Employee Stock Options** section outlines the size and the vesting schedule of the employee stock option pool. The employee stock options are a pool of authorized shares that have not been issued yet but will be issued when the employees holding the options decide to exercise the options.

Right of First Refusal/Right of Co-Sale is a tag-along or take-me-along right similar to the Right to Participate Pro Rata in Future Rounds. The difference is in the source of the shares being acquired by the investors under the rights. In the case of future rounds, the company is issuing new shares, which the investors can purchase up to a maximum of pro rata to their existing shareholdings. In the right of first refusal (ROFR), the founders and other key employees are selling their existing shares, all of which can be purchased pro rata by the existing investors. As example of a ROFR case is a founder leaving the company and tendering his or her shares; the existing investors will have the right to purchase these shares.

The **Board of Directors** section outlines the make-up of the board.

The **Drag Along right** is a right that allows, say, a majority shareholder of the company to force a minority shareholder to join in a liquidation event, such as the sale of the company. For example, if the more than 50% of the shareholders approve a sale of the company and the founder does not agree, this clause can be used to force the founder to sell his or her shares at the same price, terms, and conditions as the remaining shareholders. This forced "drag along" sale can allow the company to be sold to a buyer looking to acquire all shares of the company – that is, not a partial stake.

The **Founders' Stock** section outlines the restrictions set out on the shares issued to the founder(s) outright – that is, shares issued to compensate for past work or for "founding" the company. The restrictions make the founder(s) stay with the company or risk losing those shares as the company can buy them back at cost – a nominal amount. These restrictions lapse over time, however.

The **No Shop/Confidentiality** terms are standard confidentiality provisions designed to prevent "shopping around" once the terms have been accepted by both parties. Finally, **Expiration** provides a timeline for accepting the terms contained in the term sheet.

LIQUIDATION PREFERENCE

In a previous chapter, we discussed the preferential nature of the preferred shares issued by the company. The **Liquidation Preference** section details the terms and mechanics of how the preferences will work if a liquidation event takes place (including a merger or a sale).

For example, for a non-participating preferred share, the preference is defined as the purchase price plus declared dividends. For participating preferred share, the preference is still defined as the purchase price plus declared dividends, but the aspect of subsequent pro rata sharing with common shares is also defined.

Increasingly, the term sheets are doing away with liquidation preferences of more than 1X, but it is still not uncommon to find a deal where the liquidation preference is, say, 2X or 3X. This multiple means that if the purchase price was $10 per share, the preference would be for $20 or $30 per share – and <u>not</u> for $10 per share.

ANTI-DILUTION PROVISIONS

Suppose you are enrolled in a private equity course with a major group project due at the end. Suppose your professor tells you that you can submit the project ahead of time and receive a high score. You spend a gallant effort on the project and submit it early even though some of the content of the subsequent lectures could have been helpful if you had waited. How would you feel if someone else submitted the project at the very end up with help from the subsequent lecture notes and actually secured higher marks than you?

The concept of anti-dilution is very similar. You invest early but, of no fault of your own, have to suffer a reduction in the value of your shares just because someone else decided to wait and invest later. You want the management team to grow the value of the company with your investment; if the management team makes poor decisions, it should make you whole when the subsequent valuation goes lower.

Suppose a venture capitalist buys 10,000 shares of a company in the first round at a price of $5 per share for a total investment of $50,000. (Before the investment, the company already had 30,000 common shares outstanding.) We will call this venture capitalist the Round 1 VC. Unfortunately, the company suffers a market share loss due to the management team's poor decisions and the company's value goes down. In the second round, a new venture capitalist (Round 2 VC) buys 5,000 shares of the company at a price of $3 per share. The first venture capitalist would like protection against the subsequent dilution and wants to put in the term sheet certain **anti-dilution** provisions to protect the value of its shares.

There are two choices: **full-ratchet** protection and **weighted average** protection. We discuss the two below.

FULL-RATCHET PROTECTION

Under a full-ratchet protection, the price of Round 1 VC's shares is reduced to equal that of the Round 2 VC's shares. In the example above, the Round 1 VC will end up with a share price of $3 per share as well. However, because the share certificates have already been issued in amounts determined in Round 1, the pricing accommodation provided to the Round 1 VC is achieved by modifying the conversion price of those preferred shares.

Recall that the conversion feature of the preferred shares, if present, allows them to be converted into common shares if there is a liquidation event such as an IPO, a sale, and so on, or an attached conversion right. If, in the example above, each Round 1 preferred share converts into one common share at a conversion price of $5 per share, the $50,000 Round 1 investment would convert into 10,000 common shares <u>without</u> any anti-dilution protection.

$$\$50,000 \, / \, \$5 = 10,000 \text{ common shares}$$

Under the full-ratchet protection, conversion price would change to $3 per share such that the $50,000 Round 1 investment would convert into 16,667 common shares with the protection.

$$\$50,000 \, / \, \$3 = 16,667 \text{ common shares}$$

Effectively, the cost of the Round 1 preferred shares on a converted basis is now $3 per share.

WEIGHTED-AVERAGE PROTECTION

Under the weighted average protection, the pricing logic is very similar except that instead of lowering the price to $3 per share, an adjustment is made to account for the relative sizes of the two rounds. That is, the Round 1 conversion price is not lowered all the way down to $3 per share because fewer than 10,000 shares have been issued in Round 2. You consider the weighted average of the shares issued in the two rounds relative to the original shares.

The formula is:

$$CP_{Modified} = CP_{Original} * \frac{[\, N_{Prior} + (\text{New Investment} / CP_{Original}) \,]}{[\, N_{Prior} + \text{New shares issued} \,]}$$

Where:
    $CP_{Modified}$ = conversion price of the original shareholders after the new investment
    $CP_{Original}$ = conversion price of the original shareholders before the new investment
    N_{Prior} = number of shares outstanding before the new investment
    New investment = total investment made or funds raised in the new round
    New shares issued = total number of shares issued in the new round

In our example above, we get the modified conversion price using the following inputs:

$CP_{Original} = \$5$
$N_{Prior} = 30,000 + 10,000 = 40,000$
New investment $= \$3 * 5,000 = \$15,000$
New shares issued $= 5,000$

Therefore:

$$CP_{Modified} = \$5 * [\ 40,000\ + (\$15,000\ /\ \$5)\ ]\ /\ [\ 40,000 + 5,000\ ] = \$4.78$$

Again, the assumption here is that one preferred share converts into a single common share. Note that the anti-dilution protection in this case is only invoked if the share price in a subsequent round is lower than that in the previous round. The anti-dilution protection formula cannot increase the conversion price (as the formula will not be invoked).

MANAGEMENT CARVE-OUTS

In recessionary or crises times or following dilutive financings, the management team and/or the founders of an early-stage company may be left with insufficient equity in the company to keep them motivated. In other cases, the VC's liquidation preferences may become inadvertently punishing over the course of time. To solve this motivational issue, the investors and the management team/founders may agree on a **management carve-out** which allows the management team/founders to receive a preferential distribution (usually 5-10%) in addition to their common equity.

For example, suppose the founders own 30% of the equity of the company in the form of common shares, but, due to troubling economic environment, subsequent financings have placed several preferences on top of their common shares. If the company is sold for $100 MM, the liquidation preferences of the investors will not leave any funds to be distributed to the founders. The investors can motivate the founders by allowing them a meaningful 5% carve-out in the form of preferred shares having the same liquidation preference as the investors.

The carve-outs can be negotiated to any extent and in any form. For instance, any preferences allowed to the founders under a carve-out can be offset against their common shares in case the company is sold for a much higher valuation and the common shares become valuable.

A company is worth $500 MM today. The capital structure, in the order of preference, is:

- Zero-coupon debt of $10 MM face value, currently yielding 5% to maturity (which is in two years' time)
- 50,000 Series B preferred shares, liquidation preference of 2X the face value, participating with a limit of 4X the face value, face value of $1,000 per share, 6% cumulative dividend rate, issued two years ago
- 50,000 Series A preferred shares, participating, face value of $500 per share, 8% cumulative dividend rate, issued three years ago
- 100,000 common shares

Additionally, the venture debt has a total of 50,000 warrants associated with it, with each warrant giving the debt holder the right to purchase one common share at a price of $500 per share. The warrants can be exercised today.

If redeemed, the preferential proceeds to each category of shares will also include any declared but unpaid dividends. No dividend has ever been paid in the company's history on any share. If the company is liquidated today, calculate the total proceeds to be received by each category of shares.

A company is worth $650 MM today. The capital structure, in the order of preference, is:

- Zero-coupon debt of $20 MM face value, currently yielding 5% to maturity (which is in three years' time)
- 50,000 Series B preferred shares, liquidation preference of 3X the face value, participating, face value of $1,000 per share, 6% cumulative dividend rate, issued two years ago
- 40,000 Series A preferred shares, convertible into one common share each, face value of $1,000 per share, 8% cumulative dividend rate, issued four years ago
- 80,000 common shares

Additionally, the venture debt has a total of 100,000 warrants associated with it, with each warrant giving the debt holder the right to purchase one common share at a price of $400 per share. The warrants can be exercised today.

If redeemed, the preferential proceeds to each category of shares will also include any declared but unpaid dividends. No dividend has ever been paid in the company's history on any share. If the company is liquidated today, calculate the total proceeds to be received by each category of shares.

A company is worth $500 MM today. The capital structure, in the order of preference, is as follows:

- Zero-coupon debt of $10 MM face value, currently yielding 5% to maturity (which is in two years' time)
- 50,000 Series B preferred shares, liquidation preference of 2X the face value, participating with a limit of 4X the face value, face value of $500 per share, face value of $1,000, 6% cumulative dividend rate, issued two years ago
- 50,000 Series A preferred shares, participating, face value of $1,000 per share, 8% cumulative dividend rate, issued three years ago
- 100,000 common shares

Additionally, the venture debt has a total of 50,000 warrants associated with it, with each warrant giving the debt holder the right to purchase one common share at a price of $500 per share. The warrants can be exercised today.

If redeemed, the preferential proceeds to each category of shares will also include any declared but unpaid dividends. No dividend has ever been paid in the company's history on any share. If the company is liquidated today, calculate the total proceeds to be received by each category of shares, under the following two independent assumptions:

(A) Series A preferred shares have a full-ratchet anti-dilution protection; and
(B) Series A preferred shares have a weighted-average anti-dilution protection.

A company is worth $650 MM today. The capital structure, in the order of preference, is as follows:

- Zero-coupon debt of $20 MM face value, currently yielding 5% to maturity (which is in three years' time)
- 50,000 Series B preferred shares, liquidation preference of 3X the face value, participating, face value of $800 per share, 6% cumulative dividend rate, issued two years ago
- 40,000 Series A preferred shares, convertible into one common share each, face value of $1,000 per share, 8% cumulative dividend rate, issued four years ago
- 80,000 common shares

Additionally, the venture debt has a total of 100,000 warrants associated with it, with each warrant giving the debt holder the right to purchase one common share at a price of $400 per share. The warrants can be exercised today.

If redeemed, the preferential proceeds to each category of shares will also include any declared but unpaid dividends. No dividend has ever been paid in the company's history on any share. If the company is liquidated today, calculate the total proceeds to be received by each category of shares, under the following two independent assumptions:

(A) Series A preferred shares have a full-ratchet anti-dilution protection; and
(B) Series A preferred shares have a weighted-average anti-dilution protection.

Chapter 4

THE VENTURE INVESTMENT MODEL

A venture investment model is not a typical investment model followed in corporate finance. The model is based on the concept of **implied valuation**.

Before we can build the logic for the implied valuation method, we must recognize that a venture investment faces an ocean of uncertainty unlike any other investment in finance. The venture investment is usually intended for a very long time horizon – more than 5 years and not uncommon to approach 10 years – while not much can be forecasted with ease beyond the short term. There is a great dispersion of possible future outcomes, including the complete writeoff or loss of the investment.

Nevertheless, if there is one thing most of the parties can agree to today (that is, at the time of the investment), it is what they all want the company to become in the future. To be precise, all parties involved can foresee a future which tells of a major liquidation event once the company has accomplished a good portion of what it set out to do. An example of the liquidation event is an initial public offering (an IPO) of the company. Another example is the sale of the company to a competitor or yet another investment firm.

For earlier-stage ventures, the event may even be a follow-on investment by another venture capital firm, without the original investor actually receiving any liquidity at that time. One example is the case of the "seed" funding offered by the likes of the *Y Combinator* funds. In such cases, the investors will put in smaller amounts of capital upfront giving you enough money to make your way to the first 'regular' round, where a more traditional source of financing might be on offer from a reputable venture capital firm.

While you are no longer sure of what the future will look like, you and your fellow shareholders, including the company founders and management team, can all agree to an event in the future and an expected company value at that time if all goes according to the plan. This common understanding of the future – which will still need to be 'negotiated' and agreed upon by all involved – holds the key to building our venture investment model. Before we get into the details, however, we will review the stages of development of a new venture.

THE FOUR STAGES OF DEVELOPMENT

Most ventures can be conceptually structured into four distinct phases of growth:

- Exploration — An idea is born, validated, and nourished into an opportunity.
- Development — A product/service is developed and early customers are identified.
- Revenue — The product/service is sold on an increasing scale.
- Profit — The company operates as a profitable and growing concern.

These four stages need to be explicitly incorporated into a financial model. Each of these stages has a unique set of goals and a different set of underlying assumptions; each has a distinct cash flow profile and risk/reward ratio. Thus, all four stages need to be fully developed since they each provide a financial profile of the opportunity — the exploration and development stages (and perhaps even the revenue stage) are usually net users of scarce cash and equity; the profit stage illustrates the opportunity's upside. Investors, for example, will get a real sense of the economic value created by staging their investments to coincide with the completion of each phase.

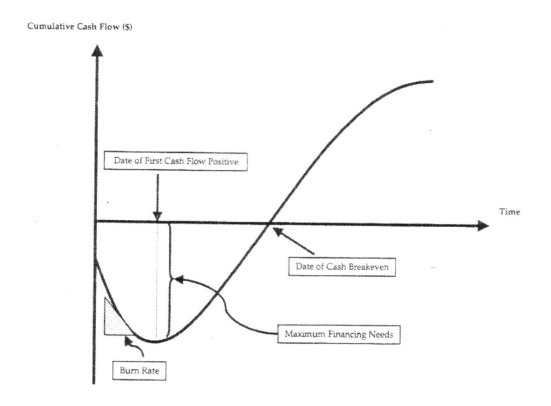

EXPLORATION

In the exploratory phase, entrepreneurs set the groundwork for pursuing an opportunity. They set up the appropriate legal structure and incorporate the venture. They typically also develop and perfect a business plan. As part of this process, they conduct preliminary market research. If possible, they build a product prototype and get feedback from potential customers.

During this phase, entrepreneurs also attract key stakeholders to their opportunity. They identify and, if possible, attract the few team members who are vital to developing the opportunity. Finally, with a business plan in hand, they attempt to raise the funds to finance the next phase, the product development.

The exploratory phase is characterized by several major risks:

- Does the market really exist for the new idea?
- Can the team develop a product that the customers will buy?'
- Can the entrepreneur assemble the right team to execute on the opportunity?
- Can the entrepreneur get his/her opportunity financed?

Traditional sources of capital for funding the exploratory stage include bootstrapping (and paying low or no wages), friends and family, potential customers, business partners, and early-stage angel investors.

DEVELOPMENT

During the development phase, the team proves that a real market exists. They develop a prototype, if not an "imperfect" final product/service, that can be sold to early adopters who are willing to test it. As the market is validated, it is critical to begin to develop the sales and marketing capabilities that will be used during the revenue phase.

Entrepreneurs also need to raise enough money for the next phase, the revenue phase. By this time, they should have assembled a Board of Directors. Typically this Board will be partially populated with key investors. More importantly, the entrepreneur must ensure that this Board is staffed with directors who possess skills that are consistent with a venture's key success factors.

The development phase has three major risks — market and product risks as well as risks associated with funding this cycle. The ultimate goal of this phase is to prove that the company can build a product and that customers will buy this product. Thus, problems may arise with the market validation and product development efforts. In many instances, start-ups are forced to literally go back to the drawing board and re-develop a product from scratch. In these cases, there may also be a team risk since new skills may be needed to develop a new product.

Typical sources of funding for the development phase include the development-stage investors as well as professional sources, such as later-stage angel investors, venture capitalists, customers, and suppliers.

REVENUE

Once the product is proven, a venture will ramp up sales. In the revenue phase, entrepreneurs typically have the goal of breaking-even from a cash flow perspective as quickly as possible.

There are several risks in the revenue phase:

- Does the company have the appropriate sales and marketing plan and can it execute it?
- Can the company scale up smoothly as revenues begin to grow aggressively?
- How will competitors react to the new product?
- Since the venture has not yet broken even, how will an entrepreneur finance a company's aggressive growth rate?

During the revenue phase, it is not unusual for a venture to use secured or unsecured financing (for example, a bank loan) rather than equity to finance its growth.

PROFIT

In this phase, a venture is profitable and may continue its aggressive growth trajectory (by, for example, focusing on market share gains) in order to maximize the value of the opportunity. To this end, a venture may decide to extend its sales channels, seek strategic alliances that can enhance its ability to sell, or launch new products/services. In addition, it may need to hire aggressively to staff its growth.

Some of the risks in the revenue phase still remain:

- Does the organization have the skills to "get to the next level?" Can the founding entrepreneurial team "scale up?"
- How will competitors react to a company that is capturing market share?

A NOTE ON ANGEL INVESTORS

One popular source of early-stage equity capital is private investors, also known as **"angel" investors** (or, simply, "angels"). These investors may range from family and friends with a few extra dollars to extremely wealthy individuals who manage their own money. Successful entrepreneurs frequently come to mind, and do, in fact, represent a significant source of private funding.

Angels may be advised by their accountants, lawyers or other professionals, and sometimes the entrepreneur must deal with these people as well. In the late 1990s, a new form of angel financing evolved. Individual angels grouped together and tried to invest more formally: recruiting members with specialized expertise (typically former or current entrepreneurs, retired venture capitalists, and so on), sharing due diligence and contacts, structuring more formal and sophisticated financing terms, and involving themselves more deeply in the company (such as through a board seat).

One of the best ways to find angel investors is through a network of friends, acquaintances, and advisors. For instance, if you have used a local lawyer and accountant to help you prepare a business plan or offering document, these advisors may know of wealthy individuals who invest in ventures like yours.

IMPLICATIONS OF THE FOUR STAGES OF DEVELOPMENT

Each of the four stages requires different resources for the business and each has distinct risks and rewards. This has major implications for how an entrepreneur should go about raising capital (especially equity).

Entrepreneurs should consider staging capital investments to coincide with the completion of a stage, especially in the exploratory and development stages (and to a lesser extent the revenue stage). The successful completion of each stage marks the elimination of major risks and the successful validation of several dimensions of the opportunity. As such, the valuation of the company should correspondingly increase. The reduction of risk that occurs at each stage results in a higher valuation for the venture and a corresponding lower internal rate of return to attract the necessary capital. Thus, by staging equity capital, an entrepreneur will minimize the equity dilution created by a round of financing. The staging of equity also allows the entrepreneur to choose the right type of value added partners at each stage.

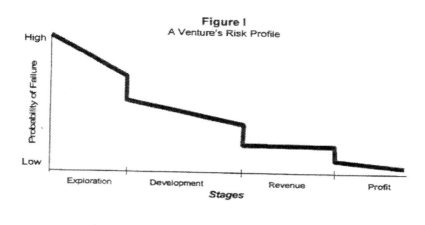

Figure I
A Venture's Risk Profile

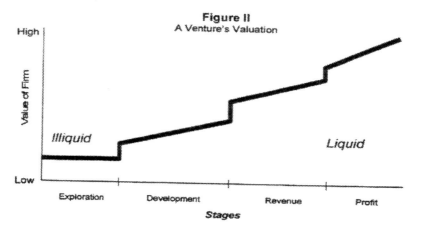

Figure II
A Venture's Valuation

While staging is very common in early-stage investments, it is important to understand the reasons behind choosing it as well as the risks that it entails. Refer to the table below for more detailed insights.

STAGING	Pros	Cons
Entrepreneurs	<ul><li>In a venture with a successful trajectory, staging will minimize dilution for existing equity holders.</li><li>Staging allows entrepreneur to choose new investors (and partners) in the future.</li></ul>	<ul><li>In a venture with a "rocky" trajectory, staging may lead to increased dilution due to "down" rounds.</li><li>Staging of capital may be considered imprudent since no one can guarantee availability of equity capital in the future.</li><li>Staging capital requires more rounds of financing. Thus, the entrepreneur needs to spend more time raising money. This is not appropriate if the total amount of money needed for the venture is relatively small.</li></ul>
Investors	<ul><li>Staging allows investors to avoid making "all or nothing" bets (as they can stage equity as risk/reward ratio improves).</li><li>It essentially provides an option and knowledge to prudently invest in the next stage.</li><li>Staging allows investors to get comfortable with a venture's team.</li><li>In a venture with a successful trajectory, staging requires investors to pay more for a given level of equity.</li></ul>	<ul><li>In a venture with a successful trajectory, staging requires investors to pay more for a given level of equity.</li></ul>

PRE- AND POST-MONEY VALUATIONS

Pre-money valuation is the valuation of the company *immediately before* the funds are invested in the company. **Post-money valuation** is the valuation of the company *immediately after* the funds are invested in the company. Both valuations are implied, based on the 'money' being invested, and measured at the same point in time.

For example, suppose a venture capitalist (VC) firm is investing $5 MM in a company in return for a 50% ownership. This set of facts would imply that the pre-VC shareholders will own the other 50% of the company and that the VC's 50%-owned portion of the company is worth $5 MM at the time of the investment. Now, because all shares of the same class have the same market value per share at any given point in time, it means that the pre-VC shareholders' 50%-owned portion is also worth $5 MM at the time of the investment. The pre-money value of the company is $5 MM (pre-VC shareholders' equity value) and the post-money value of the company is $10 MM (pre-VC shareholders' and VC's combined equity value).

Pre-money Valuation $5 MM	New 'Money' $5 MM

Post-money Valuation of $10 MM

If there are both preferred and common shares in the capital structure, the preferred shareholders' equity stake will be expressed in terms of the common shares that the preferred shares convert into.

If the company is being referred to here by way of the value of its equity, the pre- and post-money valuations will also be the valuations of the equity. On the other hand, if the valuations are those of the overall firm, then the valuations are those of the overall firm as well. In this text, unless otherwise stated, we will reserve the pre-and post-money valuation definitions to those of equity only.

MARKET CAPITALIZATION AND ENTERPRISE VALUE

As before, basic market capitalization of the company is defined as the number of shares outstanding times the price per share. The fully diluted market capitalization is defined as fully diluted shares times the price per share. Market capitalization is sometimes reserved for the public-market version of the market value of equity.

The **enterprise value (EV)** is defined as follows:

$$EV = \text{Market Capitalization} + \text{Market Value of Debt} - \text{Cash and Cash Equivalents}$$

Where:

- **EV** = Enterprise Value = Firm's overall value (sometimes also referred to as Total Enterprise Value or TEV)

- **Debt** = All securities issued by the firm that are not common shares and include bank debt, bonds, notes, loans, plain vanilla preferred shares, minority interests, and other similar securities

- **Cash and cash equivalents** = Cash and cash-equivalent balance held by the company that is available to the entire firm and is not restricted

Note that all values above are calculated as of the same date. The mix of equity, debt, and cash specific to a firm is known as its **capital structure**.

CAPITALIZATION TABLES

Capitalization tables (also known as "**cap tables**") are used to record and track ownership in a company. Think of them as the shareholders' equity section of a balance sheet with the added detail of investors or rounds and of market values and share prices. While debt is not directly included in the cap tables, any equity portion of the debt – such as that of convertible debt – is. Cap tables are based on fully diluted shareholdings – so, any stock options would also affect the calculations.

A sample **post-money** cap table is produced below. The 'money' event here is the Series B Preferred round.

Shareholders	Investment	Cost per Share	No. of Shares	Preference	Ownership %
Founders	$0	$0.00	2,000,000	Common	30.8%
Key employees	$0	$0.00	1,000,000	Common	15.4%
Angel group	$500,000	$0.50	1,000,000	Common	15.4%
Series A Preferred	$3,000,000	$2.00	1,500,000	Participating preferred	23.0%
Series B Preferred	$5,000,000	$5.00	1,000,000	Participating preferred	15.4%
Total			**6,500,000**		**100.0%**

The ownership % is calculated as the number of shares owned divided by the total number of shares. For example, 15.4% = 1,000,000 / 6,500,000.

The cap table above would have the following **pre-money** equivalent:

Shareholders	Investment	Cost per Share	No. of Shares	Preference	Ownership %
Founders	$0	$0.00	2,000,000	Common	36.4%
Key employees	$0	$0.00	1,000,000	Common	18.2%
Angel group	$500,000	$0.50	1,000,000	Common	18.2%
Series A Preferred	$3,000,000	$2.00	1,500,000	Participating preferred	27.2%
Total			**5,500,000**		**100.0%**

More detail can be added to a cap table, such as the current price per share and, in the case of a liquidation event, an exit valuation and distribution of proceeds.

STEPS IN MODELLING VENTURE INVESTMENTS

Suppose a VC firm wants to invest $ 5 MM in a company that will have $10 MM in sales and $6 MM in EBITDA in six years from today. The investment will be made today with an investment horizon of five years.

Step One: Start with an exit valuation of the company as determined using an appropriate valuation method.

We start with the forecasted exit event. The exit event is usually an initial public offering, a sale of the company, or another liquidation event. The exit valuation can be determined using an appropriate valuation method, such as the application of exit multiples. Suppose the VC firm reviews a list of comparable companies, applies the appropriate private valuation adjustments, and determines that an exit multiple of a 5X EV to forward EBITDA is warranted. (The use of a forward year-6 multiple is consistent with the use of a forward earnings measure to inform our exit valuation.)

Thus, the company's enterprise value is expected to be $30 MM (= the multiple of 5 times $6 MM of EBITDA in year 6) in five years from today. Since there is no debt, the exit market capitalization will equal the exit EV in five years from today assuming there is no cash on the balance sheet at that time. This 'no cash' assumption may not be realistic in practice because if the company is profitable by then, it will also have generated some cash on the balance sheet. Note that we could have used alternative valuation measures such as NPV to calculate the value in five years from today.

Step Two: Discount the exit market capitalization to the time of investment using the VC firm's required rate of return

We know what the VC firm requires from this investment in terms of a rate of return. The next logical step is to discount the exit market capitalization to the time of investment (that is, today) using that rate. The resulting present value will equal the post-money equity valuation at the time of investment.

Suppose the VC firm in our example above requires a 20% rate of return. The present value of $30 MM discounted over a five-year investment horizon at 20% is $12.06 MM. Thus, the post-money equity valuation of the company today is $12.06 MM.

Step Three: Obtain the pre-money equity valuation and assign percentage shareholdings

To obtain the pre-money equity valuation, subtract the money being invested from the post-money equity valuation. The portion of the post-money valuation represented by the money being invested is the VC firm's equity portion, while the pre-money part belongs to the rest of the shareholders.

In our example above, $7.06 MM (= $12.06 MM - $5 MM) is the pre-money valuation of the company. The VC firm now owns $5 / $12.06 = 41.5% of the equity, while the original shareholders now own the remaining 58.5%. Note that the money being raised will be used to fund some of the negative cash flows in the future and as such will affect the accumulation of cash on the balance sheet by the time of the exit. A careful analysis of the free cash flows to the firm and to the equity can take care of this issue.

Step Four: Calculate the realized returns at the time of the exit using the realized exit valuation

The first three steps work on the premise of cash flow and earnings forecasts as expected at the time of the investment. In reality, the exit valuation and time horizon may be very different from what is forecasted at the time of the investment.

Suppose, in our example above, the actual realized exit valuation is $40 MM in four years from the time of investment. The VC firm will receive 41.5% of $40 MM = $16.6 MM, while the original shareholders will receive the remaining $23.4 MM. The VC firm's realized returns will be $(\$16.6 / \$5)^{(1/4)} - 1 = 35\%$ approximately.

PROBLEM 4.1

DRM Partners invest $3 MM for a 30% equity stake in Company A.

DRM Partners invest $4 MM for a 45% equity stake in Company B.

DRM Partners invest $580,000 for 29.65% equity stake in Company C.

Calculate the pre- and post-money equity valuations of each of the three companies.

PROBLEM 4.2

A company is worth $450 MM today. The capital structure, in the order of preference, is as follows:

- 50,000 Series C preferred shares, convertible into one common share each, face value of $1,000
- 40,000 Series B preferred shares, participating, face value of $1,000 per share
- 20,000 Series A preferred shares, participating, face value of $500 per share
- 90,000 common shares

If redeemed, the preferential proceeds to each category of shares will equal their face values. All declared dividends have already been paid. Build the pre- and post-money cap tables at the time of the Series C investment.

PROBLEM 4.3

A company is worth $600 MM today. The capital structure, in the order of preference, is as follows:

- 50,000 Series C preferred shares, convertible into one common share each, face value of $1,000 per share, 5% cumulative dividend rate, issued one year ago
- 50,000 Series B preferred shares, participating, face value of $800 per share, 6% cumulative dividend rate, issued two years ago
- 25,000 Series A preferred shares, participating, face value of $600 per share, 8% cumulative dividend rate, issued four years ago
- 90,000 common shares

If redeemed, the preferential proceeds to each category of shares will equal their face values plus any declared but unpaid dividends. No dividend has ever been paid in the company's history on any share. Build the pre- and post-money cap tables at the time of the Series C investment.

PROBLEM 4.4

You are a venture capitalist, and you require a 30% rate of return on your venture investments. The following comparable company information is provided as of December 31, 2012, for the investment you are about to make.

Company	Share Price	Shares (MM)	Debt ($ MM)	Cash ($ MM)	2012 EBITDA ($ MM)	2013 EBITDA ($ MM)
Comp A	$5.50	320	255	17	330	349
Comp B	$24.25	455	1,047	237	1,883	2,038
Comp C	$19.58	505	105	256	1,629	1,685

Using the average EV-to-forward-EBITDA multiple for exit valuation, a 20% size discount on exit, and a 5-year investment horizon, calculate the minimum equity ownership that you should negotiate for a $5 MM investment today if the company's EBITDA in the 6th year from today is forecasted to be $12 MM?

PROBLEM 4.5

You are a venture capitalist, and you require a 40% rate of return on your venture investments. The following comparable company information is provided as of December 31, 2012, for the investment you are about to make.

Company	Share Price	Shares (MM)	Debt ($ MM)	Cash ($ MM)	2012 Sales ($ MM)	2013 Sales ($ MM)
Comp A	$5.50	320	255	17	801	838
Comp B	$24.25	455	1,047	237	4,537	4,967
Comp C	$19.58	505	105	256	3,888	4,051

Using the average EV-to-forward-sales multiple for exit valuation, a 25% control premium on exit, and a 6-year investment horizon, calculate the minimum equity ownership that you should negotiate for a $5 MM investment today if the company's sales in the 7th year from today is forecasted to be $21 MM?

Chapter 5

AN INTRODUCTION TO LEVERAGED BUYOUTS

© Adeel Mahmood, 2012

A **leveraged buyout (LBO)** is buying out a company with an above-average level of financial leverage. When we speak of high financial leverage, we refer to the level of debt in the capital structure that is more than the conventional levels of debt for that company or industry. The level of debt can be quantified using measures such as the debt-to-equity ratio or the interest coverage ratio. High levels of financial leverage increase the expected return and the risk of achieving that return. When the returns are highly financially leveraged, the risk of financial distress becomes much higher mainly because the increased financial burden on the company to maintain and service that level of debt which is contractually fixed in several ways.

Due to the excessive financial burden to maintain and service a high level of debt, a company should not take on such levels of high financial leverage unless it can minimize the risk of the associated financial distress. As a result, you normally do not see public-market companies, which seek to maintain a steady capital structure, take on high levels of debt. Private companies, however, are only answerable to their private shareholders and, thus, a leveraged buyout for a company taken or kept private becomes a possibility.

As soon as a leveraged buyout is complete, the company has its task cut out: that is, lower the risk of and eventually avoid financial distress with a superior, careful, and watchful cash flow management. Accordingly, the companies best suited for a leveraged buyout normally have the following common features:

- Predictable cash flows and earnings;
- Operating in industries that are not undergoing adverse events;
- Operating in industries that do not require high levels of capital expenditures to sustain or grow cash flows;
- Capacity to take on additional debt without adverse consequences; and so on.

As is clear from this discussion, debt takes the center stage of a leveraged buyout and a watchful management of the company's operations is necessary to mitigate the resulting high risk of financial distress. If all goes as per the plan, a proportionally high·financial return awaits the investors at the end.

THE THEORY OF LEVERAGED BUYOUTS

Recall the WACC curve from your basic corporate finance course. (Note that WACC refers to the weighted average cost of capital.) Initially, when there is no debt in the capital structure, the WACC is the same as the cost of equity. There are no tax shield benefits because there are none to be had from an equity-only capital structure. A good corporate finance strategy would be to take on debt at this time because the cost of debt (that is, the interest expense) is tax deductible. This is in contrast with dividends or other forms of returns provided to the equity shareholders, which are not tax-deductible. Therefore, the more debt you take on, the more the benefits of tax shield and the higher the value of the firm.

However, as you take on more debt, you also take on the increased risk of financial distress such that there comes a point where the increased benefits of tax shield are offset by the increased costs of financial stress. At this point, the company has an optimal capital structure. (Beyond the optimal capital structure, the cost of financial distress overwhelms the benefits of the tax shield.) Most public companies, if given a choice, would operate with the debt level below that implied by the optimal capital structure. Such conservative capital structure is prudent in case the company needs to raise more funds, say, for a new acquisition or a new project or if the funds are needed in the short term.

In a leveraged buyout scenario, when you take on more debt, you take it well beyond that implied in the optimal capital structure. You are after the promised high return, but to counter the associated level of high financial distress, you need to instill a very exact and detailed discipline on the management and operations of that company. From the time of the buyout till the exit, the company will be paying down debt. It will begin its journey towards the optimal capital structure, pass through it, and end up at a level of debt which is in line with what comparable public companies would have at the time of exit.

Therefore, you can think of the leveraged buyout returns as the leveraged public-market returns with a proportionally higher risk of financial distress which must be managed with a superior, careful, and watchful cash flow management.

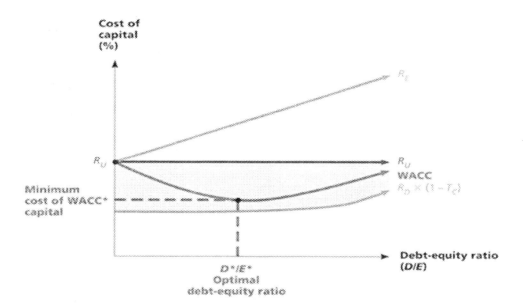

The one problem, however, is that the leverage calculations you can make to identify a potential buyout candidate can be made by just about everyone else in the market, including your target company. As a result, you will have to do better than buy the company at its current market value as the target company's shareholders will demand a higher price because they know you can pay more due to higher possible returns. Negotiations will ensue, and the buyer will most likely end up paying a premium price above the market price (with the premium known as the **buyout premium**), justified because of your ability to control the company and modify its capital structure freely. The source of the control is the seats on the board of directors.

In the recent history, the **buyout premiums** have ranged from 20% to more than 100% as competition among an increasingly large number of private equity buyers has grown to scoop up an increasingly shrinking number of attractive targets. Historically, the largest premiums have been observed in expansionary times when the perceived risk of financial distress is lower in the eyes of the buyer. As the understanding of leveraged buyouts among the market participants increases, it becomes more difficult to buy a company out solely on the coat tails of financial leverage. That is, you need to pull more tricks out of your hat to outbid the buyout competition.

Now, after the buyout, you likely will not have a lot of money to spend on capital expenditures - that is, the growth engine - because you will need the money to pay down the debt. So what other tricks can you pull out your hat? Here are some examples.

- You can recruit a superior management team that can carry out your plan without any hiccups;
- Although you cannot grow revenues aggressively directly, if you also control other companies with which this company can have cross selling opportunities or synergies in strategy and operations, you may be able to do so indirectly;
- You can still lower your expenses by optimizing and streamlining your operations and cutting out unnecessary costs that could not previously be eliminated because of a lack of control;
- A reprieve from public company disclosures and onerous regulations can allow you to focus your strategy on a longer term investment horizon and, along the way, save on some of those public reporting costs; and so on.

In most cases, you as a buyer will experience a multiples contraction from the investment to the exit. That is to say, the multiple you'll pay to buy out the company will most likely be higher than the multiple you will receive upon exit, especially if you exit in public markets, for instance, by way of an IPO. There are two main reasons for this contraction in multiples.

When you buy the company, you pay a buyout premium. When you exit in public markets, however, the public market shareholders will no longer be able to exercise control over the company and, thus, will be unwilling to pay any premium. Even if you sell to another buyout firm, that firm is most likely unwilling to pay the same premium that you paid because that firm may not modify the current course of the company much as there is not much more left to do.

Because your hands are tied when it comes to spending on capital expenditures, you are unlikely to experience the same level of growth in sales that a public company without the debt burden can. By the time you sell the company, you will have most likely decreased the growth rate of the company, which will have a direct impact on the multiples.

There are, however, ways to counter the **multiples contraction**. For example, you can sell the company to strategic buyer who normally is willing to pay a higher premium than either a financial buyer like you or the public market shareholders. Also, you can time your investment and exit to coincide favourably with the levels of multiples in the market. For instance, you can buy when the markets are depressed (that is, overall multiples are lower) and sell when the markets are bullish (that is, overall multiples are higher). Keep in mind, however, that if you need to wait to find a bullish market, the wait will have a direct effect on your returns.

DIFFERENT LAYERS OF DEBT AND VALUE CREATION

As discussed above, the value of the firm will increase as debt is paid down to achieve an optimal capital structure. Since equity (earned through free cash flows) displaces debt, the equity value of the company increases.

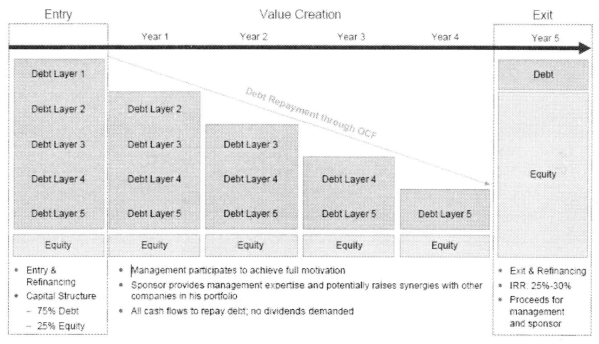

Source: (Citigroup corporate and investment banking 2006)

The pictorial representation may be oversimplified. In reality, the seniority of the debt may not have such a direct relationship with the term of the debt.

The different debt layers in an LBO deal represent the various sources of debt ranging from high-cost debt such as high-yield notes in junior debt layers to low-cost financing such as a revolving credit facility and term loans in more senior layers. The **revolving credit facility** (known as the "**revolver**") acts much like a line of credit.

The debt part of the LBO financing structure often includes a broad array of loans, securities or other debt instruments with varying terms and conditions that appeal to different classes of investors. Needless to say, the financing structure is unique to each deal. Each credit facility is negotiated given the specific deal and, thus, the cost and size of the different facilities are never the same. There still are, however, similarities in financing structures among most buyouts.

A typical LBO structure comprises the following sources of funds:

- Senior debt or first-lien secured debt such as a revolving credit facility and term loan facilities;
- Mezzanine debt, ranked between traditional debt and equity;
- High-yield corporate bonds; and
- Equity contribution, the lowest ranked and, thus, the most expensive source of funds.

SENIOR DEBT

Senior debt is the primary financing source in an LBO and typically has a term of 5 to 10 years. It consists of bank loans with a higher ranking, lower flexibility, and, thus, lower cost of capital than other sources of funds. Interest rate is typically LIBOR plus a spread of 2-3% with the credit spread tied to the credit rating of the company as well as the appraised fair market value of assets that can be used as collateral. However, to hedge the interest-rate exposure, interest-rate swaps may be used in the capital structure.

Senior debt is still flexible with varying collateral and covenant packages as well as amortization schedules. It often comprises of 25-50% of the total deal. The debt is normally collateralized with property, equipment, and other tangible assets. Main lenders are commercial and investment banks, mutual funds, structured investment funds, and finance companies.

Revolver

A traditional cash flow revolving credit facility also called "**revolver**" is a senior debt secured by inventory and accounts receivable (that is, the most liquid non-cash current assets). It is a line of credit extended by a (syndicate of) bank(s) that permits the borrower to draw varying amounts up to a specified aggregate limit for a specified period of time – which may be 5 years or more.

Like a typical line of credit, the amounts borrowed can be freely repaid and re-borrowed during the term of the facility. A revolver requires the borrower to maintain a certain credit profile through compliance with financial covenants contained in the credit agreement. It is common for companies to utilize a revolver or equivalent lending arrangements to provide ongoing liquidity for seasonal working capital needs, letters of credit, and other general corporate purposes. A revolver, however, is normally not used to fund the purchase of the target company in an LBO and is usually undrawn on entry or exit.

Revolvers are typically arranged by one or more investment banks and then syndicated to a group of commercial banks and finance companies. While the cost of a revolver is in line with the senior term debt, a nominal annual commitment fee is charged on the undrawn portion of the facility. This fee compensates the lenders for making the line of credit available to the borrower, much like other lines of credit where the borrower has the option but not an obligation to exercise the borrowing rights.

Term Loans

A **term loan** is a loan for a specific amount that has a specified repayment schedule and a floating interest rate (such as the one based on LIBOR). Term loans normally mature within 10 years.

A traditional term loan for LBO financing is structured as a first-lien debt obligation and requires the borrower to maintain a certain credit profile through compliance with financial covenants contained in the credit agreement. A term loan must be fully funded on the date of closing and once principal is repaid, it cannot be re-borrowed. Term loans are classified by an identifying letter such as A, B, C, and so on, to reflect their lender base, amortization schedules, and terms.

Term Loan A ("TLA")

TLAs are commonly referred to as amortizing term loan because they typically require substantial principal repayment throughout their life. Term loans with significant annual required amortizations are perceived by lenders as less risky as the repayment reduces the principal balance outstanding. It is no surprise, then, that TLAs are often the lowest-cost debt in the capital structure - unless if there is a mortgage secured by specific higher-quality assets. TLAs are syndicated to commercial banks and finance companies together with the revolver on a pro rata basis. TLAs in the LBO financing structure often have a term that ends simultaneously with the maximum term of the revolver.

Term Loan B ("TLB"), Term Loan C ("TLC"), and Others

TLBs, TLCs, and other sequential term loans (collectively referred to here as "TLBs") are commonly referred to as "institutional term loans" as they are sold to the institutional investor base, which has grown over the years in the United States and Europe. Typically, TLBs are larger in size and have a longer term than TLAs. The longer term is motivated by the commercial bank lenders' preference to have their debt (TLAs) mature before that (TLBs) of the institutional investors, who also would not mind matching the longer investment horizon with their longer dated liabilities.

TLBs are generally amortized (paid down) at a nominal rate such as 1% annually. The rest is repaid as a bullet at maturity. Common maturity terms for TLBs are seven to ten years.

Both the revolver and the term loans are senior debt – that is, they rank higher in seniority than the high-yield corporate bonds, mezzanine debt, and all forms of equity.

HIGH-YIELD CORPORATE BONDS

High-yield corporate bonds (also known as the **non-investment-grade**, **speculative-grade**, or **junk bonds**) are bonds rated below the investment grade. Non-investment grade is a rating of "Ba1" or below from Moody's Investor Service and "BB+" or below from Standard and Poor's.

These bonds have a higher risk of default or other adverse credit events, but typically provide higher returns than the senior debt in order to entice investors.

Typical term of the bonds is 7 to 10 years, but they mature after the senior debt with no repayments in between. These bonds are a flexible instrument that can be structured as a debt security with equity-linked features such as warrants. The bonds are often structured as 20-40% of the total deal and maybe publicly traded after the issue. The interest rate is LIBOR plus a spread which is higher than that of the senior debt. Main lenders are pension funds, insurance and finance companies, debt and mutual funds, hedge funds or other institutional and private investors.

MEZZANINE DEBT

Mezzanine debt refers to a subordinated debt that represents a claim on a company's assets which is senior only to that of the common or preferred shares. Often a more expensive financing source, the mezzanine debt is negotiated in detail under a private placement and is tailored to meet the financing needs of the specific transaction and required return of the available investors. It provides incremental capital at a cost below that of equity, which enables stretching of leverage levels and purchase price when alternative capital sources are inaccessible. Mezzanine debt has embedded equity instruments, such as warrants, attached to it.

In structuring the mezzanine debt, the company and the investors work together to avoid burdening the company with the full interest cost of such a debt. Because mezzanine lenders will seek an equity-like return, the return must be achieved through means other than simple cash interest payments. As a result, the return is sourced from a combination of the following:

- *Cash interest*: periodic payment of cash interest (floating or fixed) based on a percentage of the outstanding balance of the mezzanine debt;
- *Payable-in-kind (PIK) interest*: periodic form of interest in which the interest payment is accrued by adding to the principal balance outstanding (like a zero-coupon bond);
- *Equity ownership*: an equity stake in the form of attached warrants or a conversion feature (like a convertible bond).

Hedge funds, mezzanine funds, distressed debt funds, and other institutional investors are the most common investors in this layer of debt.

EQUITY CONTRIBUTION

The initial capital structure of an LBO deal is a function of the economic environment. For example, in 2006, the initial capital structure would typically consist of 75% debt and 25% equity (based on Citigroup investment banking research). That mix today may be 50-50 instead after the financial crisis. The required returns have also come down over the years as the availability of capital has increased and competition among buyout firms has grown. It is not uncommon to encounter a lower teen required return (that is, say, a 12% IRR) in deals today.

Theoretically, the IRR should be lower for large-sized deals because the fund managers are still receiving a large amount of compensation dollars. In practice though, fewer funds have the wherewithal to come up with the equity checks for such large deals and even then several of them may partner up to bid for one deal together (a **"club" deal**), effectively taking out any competition. Note that in order to keep cash flows maximized during the holding period, no dividends or other cash flows are typically paid out to equity holders.

The management team will typically also invest some capital in the deal, or they will receive stock options as the most significant part of their compensation, or both.

SOURCES AND USES OF FUNDS

Using the existing capital structure and the proposed capital structure after the buyout, we can put together a balance-sheet-type table that summarizes the sources and uses of funds at the time of the acquisition.

The sources are as discussed above under debt and equity layers (plus any cash already on the target's balance sheet). The traditional uses are the repayment of existing debt, payments to advisors, contractual or regulatory fees, and payments to existing shareholders (including those converting from existing options and/or bonds).

EARN-OUTS

An **earn-out** is a contractual provision stating that the seller of a business will receive future compensation based on the business achieving certain future financial goals. In an LBO exit outside of public markets, an earn-out stipulates that the selling principals and shareholders of the company are paid for the sale, following which they are contractually obligated to stay with the company through a transition period, and they are provided with the incentive to have a demonstrable effect on the company's financial performance going forward.

Achieving or exceeding a certain level of performance – criteria are typically set over a period of several years – means the selling shareholders and principals will earn a much larger profit from the sale. While earn-out is not a typical feature of an LBO exit, it may form part of a sale agreement to a strategic buyer or another LBO firm. Most earn-outs, if they exist, tie the future compensation to the level of future sales or earnings of the company. An example of an earn-out is a strategic buyer paying the LBO firm $80 MM upfront at the time of the sale and providing an incentive compensation element of 10% of the following two year's sales above $60 MM of base-level sales. If the sales in each of the following two years are $85 MM, then the LBO firm will receive an additional $5 MM (= 2 x 10% x {$85 MM - $60 MM}) from the strategic buyer.

Earn-outs are usually not commonplace in public-market exits (IPOs). Instead, lock-ups are used to restrict the pre-IPO shareholders from selling their stock until after the lapse of a minimum time period following the public-market listing.

PROBLEM 5.1

Your LBO firm is buying out TargCo, which currently has $14 MM of cash at hand, $66 MM of bonds outstanding, and 155 MM fully diluted common shares, trading at $1.15 per share. Under the buyout terms, you will pay off all of the current debt and take on the following pieces of new debt on the date of the buyout to complete the acquisition:

- **TLA**: new balance of $90 MM, interest rate of 6%, repayable in five equal annual instalments over the next five years
- **TLB**: new balance of $58 MM, interest rate of 8%, interest payable annually, 10% of the original principal balance repayable annually, the remaining principal balance repayable at the end of the six-year term
- **High-yield bonds (HYB)**: new balance of $45 MM, interest rate of 10%, interest payable annually, the entire principal balance repayable at the end of the seven-year term

You will also fund the financing fees of $8 MM, investment banking fees of $4 MM, and legal and other fees of $2 MM. You will pay a 21% buyout premium on top of the current trading price of the company's common shares.

Put together a table outlining the sources and uses of funds. Also, calculate TargCo's interest expense for the first year after the buyout.

PROBLEM 5.2

Your LBO firm is buying out Americana Inc, which currently has no cash at hand, $104 MM of bonds outstanding, and 211 MM fully diluted common shares, trading at $2.20 per share. Under the buyout terms, you will pay off all of the current debt and take on the following pieces of new debt on the date of the buyout to complete the acquisition:

- **TLA**: new balance of $155 MM, interest rate of 7%, repayable in five equal annual instalments over the next five years
- **High-yield bonds (HYB)**: new balance of $83 MM, interest rate of 9%, interest payable annually, the entire principal balance repayable at the end of the six-year term
- **PIK bonds**: Mezzanine debt of $78 MM face value, currently yielding 13% to maturity (which is in seven years' time)

You will also fund the financing fees of $8 MM, investment banking fees of $4 MM, and legal and other fees of $2 MM. You will pay a 19% buyout premium on top of the current trading price of the company's common shares.

Put together a table outlining the sources and uses of funds. Also, calculate Americana's interest expense for the first year after the buyout.

Chapter 6

THE LEVERAGED BUYOUT MODEL

© Adeel Mahmood, 2012

We will build a leveraged buyout model (an "LBO" model) in this chapter using a numerical example.

Suppose you're buying out a company on December 31, 2012, and the company has the following levels of forecasted EBITDA:

Year	EBITDA ($ MM)
2013	35.0
2014	38.5
2015	41.6
2016	46.5
2017	48.8
2018	51.0

Suppose that the annual amortization equals the capital expenditures, which are forecasted to be $5 MM annually over the next six years. The company faces a corporate tax rate of 30%.

Note that, in practice, you will most likely have to calculate the forecasted EBITDA given the financial modelling assumptions, such as sales forecasts and margin forecasts.

EXIT VALUATION

You expect to sell the company on December 31, 2017, for the median forward EV to EBITDA multiple observed for the following set of comparable companies. You will also apply a 10% size discount to the multiple you determine below.

Company	EV	2013 EBITDA
Comp A	1,885	329
Comp B	11,120	1,888
Comp C	10,105	1,675

The median EV to 2013 EBITDA multiple works out to be 5.89X. After applying the 10% discount, our required multiple becomes 5.3X. At 5.3X, the exit EV works out to be 5.3 * $51 MM = $270.3 MM. If we can figure out the level of debt net of cash on that date, we will get the market cap of the company on that date. To figure the level of debt and cash, we need to find out the cash flows to the company in the five years leading up to the exit and the manner of their use in the repayment of debt and interest.

The calculation of **free cash flows to the firm (FCFF)**, or unlevered free cash flows, is the next task at hand. Recall that:

FCFF = EBITDA
minus Unlevered Taxes
minus Working Capital Changes
minus Other Cash Adjustments
minus Capital Expenditures

For this model, assume that there are no working capital changes or other cash adjustments. In practice, you may have to forecast the working capital changes using your financial modelling assumptions. The other cash adjustments can include deferred taxes, stock option expense, amortization of financing and commitment fees, and so on. Examples of these adjustments relevant to the company can be found in the company's historical cash flow statements.

The unlevered taxes are typically calculated as EBIT * tax rate. These taxes represent the income tax expense for the company assuming no debt and, thus, no interest expense. We will incorporate the interest tax shield later in the model.

Using the information provided so far, we can put the following forecast together.

Forecast	2013	2014	2015	2016	2017	2018
EBITDA[1]	35.0	38.5	41.6	46.5	48.8	51.0
DA[2]	5.0	5.0	5.0	5.0	5.0	5.0
EBIT[3]	30.0	33.5	36.6	41.5	43.8	46.0
Unlevered taxes @ 30%	9.0	10.1	11.0	12.5	13.1	13.8
Working cap adjustments	-	-	-	-	-	-
Other cash adjustments	-	-	-	-	-	-
Capex[4]	5.0	5.0	5.0	5.0	5.0	5.0
FCFF	**21.0**	**23.5**	**25.6**	**29.1**	**30.7**	**32.2**

Notes:
1. EBITDA = Earnings before interest, taxes, depreciation, and amortization
2. DA = Depreciation and amortization
3. EBIT = Earnings before interest and taxes
4. Capex = Capital expenditures

We complete the 2018 forecast – if we are not given the EBITDA for the year after the exit – for exit valuation purposes. We, however, do not require the full cash flow forecast for 2018.

DEBT BREAKDOWN

Suppose the target company has no current cash at hand, and you will pay off all of its current debt and take on the following pieces of new debt on the date of investment to complete the acquisition of the company:

- **TLA**: maximum balance of 1X forward EBITDA, interest rate of LIBOR +2% swapped into an equivalent fixed rate, repayable in four equal annual instalments over the next four years
- **TLB**: maximum balance of 2X forward EBITDA, interest rate of LIBOR +2.5%, interest payable annually, 5% of the original principal balance repayable annually, the remaining principal balance repayable at the end of the six-year term
- **High-yield bonds (HYB)**: maximum balance of 1X forward EBITDA, fixed interest rate of 10%, interest payable annually, the entire principal balance repayable at the end of the seven-year term

The remainder of the acquisition price will be financed with your equity check.

Note that if there is a revolver involved, there will most likely be a commitment fee charged on the revolver annually. The bank(s) providing the revolver charge this fee to keep the funds available to you in case you decide to draw them down. Think of the commitment fee as the price of the option on the drawdown. This commitment fee is usually deferred and amortized with the debt, but your levered free cash flow forecast should deduct it as a cash outflow.

DEBT AMORTIZATION

Armed with the details of the debt arrangements, we now set up the debt amortization schedules. We will assume that you will take on the maximum amount of debt available given the forward EBITDA of $35 MM.

- TLA: 1X $35 MM = $35 MM taken out as debt
- TLB: 2X $35 MM = $70 MM taken out as debt
- HYB: 1X $35 MM = $35 MM taken out as debt

Suppose the LIBOR curve provided to you is as follows:

Rate	2013	2014	2015	2016	2017	2018
LIBOR	3.0%	3.2%	3.4%	3.6%	3.8%	4.0%
LIBOR + 2.0%	5.0%	5.2%	5.4%	5.6%	5.8%	6.0%
LIBOR + 2.5%	5.5%	5.7%	5.9%	6.1%	6.3%	6.5%

The equivalent fixed rate swapped into for TLA is calculated as
$[(1.05)*(1.052)*(1.054)*(1.056)](1/4) - 1 = 5.3\%$.

Accordingly, the blended annual TLA repayment will be $9.9 MM.

Thus, the debt and interest repayment schedules will be as follows:

TLA	2013	2014	2015	2016	2017	2018
Beginning balance	35.0	26.9	18.4	9.4	-	-
Annual payment	9.9	9.9	9.9	9.9	-	-
Interest expense	1.9	1.4	1.0	0.5	-	-
Principal repayment	8.1	8.5	9.0	9.4	-	-
Ending balance	**26.9**	**18.4**	**9.4**	**-**	**-**	**-**

For TLBs, the annual principal repayment will be 5% of $70 MM = $3.5 MM, and the interest payment will be based on the variable rate derived from the LIBOR curve.

TLB	2013	2014	2015	2016	2017	2018
Beginning balance	70.0	66.5	63.0	59.5	56.0	52.5
Interest expense	3.9	3.8	3.7	3.6	3.5	3.4
Principal repayment	3.5	3.5	3.5	3.5	3.5	3.5
Annual payment	7.4	7.4	7.4	7.4	7.4	7.4
Ending balance	**66.5**	**63.0**	**59.5**	**56.0**	**52.5**	**49.0**

The HYBs will only return the interest part (10% of $35 MM = $3.5 MM) over the investment horizon.

HYB	2013	2014	2015	2016	2017	2018
Beginning balance	35.0	35.0	35.0	35.0	35.0	35.0
Interest expense	3.5	3.5	3.5	3.5	3.5	3.5
Principal repayment	-	-	-	-	-	-
Annual payment	3.5	3.5	3.5	3.5	3.5	3.5
Ending balance	**35.0**	**35.0**	**35.0**	**35.0**	**35.0**	**35.0**

The **cash flow waterfall** is the process of repaying the claims of various stakeholders based on their priority in the capital structure on a periodic basis (such as annually).

If we begin with EBITDA, we know that we first have to pay the tax authorities the unlevered portion of income taxes. Then, we have to provide for working capital adjustments and other cash flow adjustments. This stop in the waterfall gives us the **cash flow from operations** (CFO).

Next, we take into account our capital expenditures needs (that is, capex requirements). Deducting the capex from the CFO gives us the free cash flow to the firm (FCFF). FCFF is entirely unlevered – that is, it does not contain any inflows or outflows on account of financial leverage. Looking at FCFF only, we cannot tell whether the company has any debt or not.

The critical phase of the waterfall lies in the calculation of **free cash flow to equity (FCFE)**, or levered free cash flow, from FCFF, keeping in mind the relative interest and repayment seniority of the different debt layers. In our example, the seniority is established as follows (in descending order):

1. TLA interest
2. TLA principal
3. TLB interest
4. TLB principal
5. HYB interest
6. HYB principal
7. Distributions to common shareholders (if allowed during the term)
8. Leftover cash retained in the company

The loan covenants in an LBO deal will restrict distributions (that is, dividends and return of capital) to the common shareholders until the loans have been completely discharged. In some instances, however, the lenders may allow a dividend to the common shareholders if they feel that their claims on the company will not be adversely affected.

Note that all interest expenses will have tax shield benefits associated with them, which we will provide for in the waterfall. If there are any PIK bonds, then the interest accrued on them is not cash interest, so while the tax shield benefit will normally still be applicable (that is, you get the deduction against taxable income), there is no cash outflow.

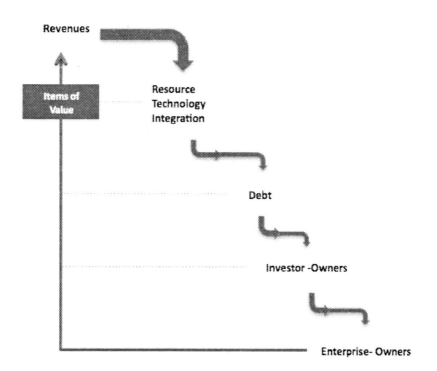

Once all layers have been 'watered', if there is still any cash leftover, it is kept on the balance sheet and accrues interest income usually at a very low rate. (The interest income and associated taxes are accounted for in the debt section – after FCFF and before FCFE). For the purposes of this example, we assume that the cash balance earns interest at a 1% rate.

If you run out of 'water' before reaching all debt layers, you will need to summon the revolver – subject to its own limits as outlined in the credit agreement. The revolver will provide you funds for making the contractual payments on various debt layers while you wait for your FCFF to grow in future years. If, of course, no new cash is forthcoming and you have drawn the revolver down fully, you will have to default on your contractual obligations and possibly seek bankruptcy protection.

It is now time to put the pieces together in our example.

Cash Flow Waterfall	2013	2014	2015	2016	2017	2018
FCFF	21.0	23.5	25.6	29.1	30.7	32.2
TLA – interest	(1.9)	(1.4)	(1.0)	(0.5)	-	-
Less: Tax shield	0.6	0.4	0.3	0.2	-	-
Subtotal	**19.7**	**22.5**	**24.9**	**28.7**	**30.7**	**32.2**
TLA – principal	(8.1)	(8.5)	(9.0)	(9.4)	-	-
Subtotal	**11.6**	**13.9**	**16.0**	**19.3**	**30.7**	**32.2**
TLB - interest	(3.9)	(3.8)	(3.7)	(3.6)	(3.5)	(3.4)
Less: Tax shield	1.2	1.1	1.1	1.1	1.1	1.0
Subtotal	**8.9**	**11.3**	**13.4**	**16.7**	**28.2**	**29.8**
TLB - principal	(3.5)	(3.5)	(3.5)	(3.5)	(3.5)	(3.5)
Subtotal	**5.4**	**7.8**	**9.9**	**13.2**	**24.7**	**26.3**
HYB - interest	(3.5)	(3.5)	(3.5)	(3.5)	(3.5)	(3.5)
Less: Tax shield	1.1	1.1	1.1	1.1	1.1	1.1
Subtotal	**3.0**	**5.3**	**7.4**	**10.8**	**22.2**	**23.9**
HYB - principal	-	-	-	-	-	-
Subtotal	**3.0**	**5.3**	**7.4**	**10.8**	**22.2**	**23.9**
Other debt payments	-	-	-	-	-	-
FCFE	**3.0**	**5.3**	**7.4**	**10.8**	**22.2**	**23.9**
Common dividends	-	-	-	-	-	-
Return of capital	-	-	-	-	-	-
Cash flow before interest income	**3.0**	**5.3**	**7.4**	**10.8**	**22.2**	**23.9**
Cash - beginning	-	3.0	8.3	15.8	26.7	49.1
Cash interest	-	0.0	0.1	0.2	0.3	0.5
Less: Taxes	-	(0.0)	(0.0)	(0.0)	(0.1)	(0.1)
New cash from business	3.0	5.3	7.4	10.8	22.2	23.9
Cash - ending	**3.0**	**8.3**	**15.8**	**26.7**	**49.1**	**73.3**

From the common shareholder's perspective, the purpose of the waterfall is simply to get the ending balances of debt and cash *immediately before* exit. Recall that we have the forecasted EV (calculated previously) waiting for us. If we can subtract debt from and add cash to the EV, we can get the market cap of the company, which represents the value of the common shares at the time of the exit.

The expected proceeds to the common shareholders at exit are:

Exit Valuation	Dec 31, 2017
Enterprise value (EV)	270.3
Less: Debt	
TLA	-
TLB	(49.0)
HYB	(35.0)
Add: Cash	49.1
***Equals*: Market cap**	**235.4**

RETURN METRICS FOR THE LBO FIRM

Two other lines also important to the common shareholders are the 'Common dividends' and 'Return of capital'. These represent cash flows to the common shareholders from the company. In this particular instance, the company is prohibited from distributing anything to the common shareholders until all debts have been paid off, which is why we see zeroes in those lines.

Note that the purchase (sale) of common shares at the time of the investment (exit) is from (to) a third party, such as a seller (buyer) or the public markets. The company and its cash flow are not involved.

Cash Flow to LBO Firm	2013	2014	2015	2016	2017
Common dividends	-	-	-	-	-
Return of capital	-	-	-	-	-
Proceeds at exit	-	-	-	-	235.4
Net cash flow	-	-	-	-	**235.4**

There are several uses of the cash flow table above.

- If the LBO firm knows amount of the equity investment it will make on December 31, 2012, it can calculate an **internal rate of return (IRR)**. For example, if the equity investment made on December 31, 2012, is $80 MM, the IRR of the net cash flows of -80, 0, 0, 0, 0, and 235.4 works out to be 24.1%. If there are no interim cash flows in the first four years, then you can also calculate the IRR as $(235.4 / 80)^{(1/5)} - 1 = 24.1\%$.

- If the LBO firm knows amount of the equity investment it will make on December 31, 2012, it can also calculate a **multiple of investment**. For example, if the equity investment made on December 31, 2012, is $80 MM and there are no interim cash flows in the first four years, then you can calculate the multiple of investment as $235.4 / 80 = 2.94$. The multiple is quick measure of the scale of profits provided; however, it does not take the time value of money into account.

- If the LBO firm knows the required return on the equity investment it will make on December 31, 2012, it can calculate the maximum equity investment it is willing to make upfront (and, thus, the maximum price it is willing to pay). For example, if the required return is 20%, then the net present value (NPV) of 0, 0, 0, 0, and 235.4 works out to be $94.6 MM, which is the maximum equity investment the firm can make on December 31, 2012.

- If the LBO firm knows the maximum equity investment it will make on December 31, 2012, it can calculate the maximum value it is willing to offer for the overall target company, including the debt. For example, if $94.6 MM is the maximum equity investment and the debt being taken on is $140.0 MM, the firm can offer $94.6 MM + $140.0 MM = $234.6 MM at maximum for the target company today (including paying off its existing creditors).

- If the existing creditors are owed $25 MM (net of the existing cash), then the firm can offer a maximum of $234.6 MM - $25.0 MM = $209.6 MM to the existing shareholders. If the existing market cap of the target company is $170.0 MM, we can calculate the **buyout premium** as (209.6 / 170.0) – 1 = 23%.

- Finally, the **profits** to the private equity fund can also be calculated given the initial investment. Suppose the LBO firm will charge a total of $10MM of management fees over the course of the investment. If the initial equity investment is $94.6 MM, we can calculate the profits to the fund as $235.4 MM - $94.6 MM - $10 MM = $130.8 MM. Assuming a performance fee or carried interest of 20%, the LBO firm will keep 20% of $130.8 MM = $26.2 MM as its compensation (in addition to the $10 MM it already received as the management fee).

Today is the morning of Jan 1, 2011. You are provided the following financial information of Shoppers Inc ("Shoppers") for the years ended Dec 31, 2009 (fiscal year 2009) and Dec 31, 2010 (fiscal year 2010):

For the Year Ended	Dec 31, 2009	Dec 31, 2010
Sales	$4,400	$4,532
Operating expenses	2,850	2,907
EBITDA	**1,550**	**1,625**
Depreciation	230	235
EBIT	**1,320**	**1,390**
Interest expense	-	-
Income before taxes	**1,320**	**1,390**
Income tax expense	396	417
Net income	**924**	**973**

Shoppers currently has no debt and only a negligible amount of cash at hand.

JLR Partners ("JLR"), a private equity firm, has agreed to purchase today all outstanding shares of Shoppers for a total amount of $11,200. However, JLR will pay only a portion of this amount using its own cash (as equity), as the remainder will be financed by a loan from an independent bank and secured by Shoppers' assets.

The loan will have a three-year term, a market value today equal to the face value, and a fixed coupon rate of 8%. The amount of loan provided by the bank will be set such that the 2011 Operating income (EBIT) will be exactly double the amount of the resulting before-tax 2011 interest expense. However, regardless of the ratio of Operating income to Interest expense, the amount of loan as a percentage of total purchase price cannot exceed 85%.

Suppose all cash flows occur at year ends. For 2011 onwards, assume that:
- Sales will grow at the same annual sales growth rate as that between 2009 and 2010;
- Operating expenses will grow at the inflation rate of 2%;
- Depreciation will be at the same dollar level as in 2010;
- Capital expenditures will equal depreciation;
- There will no working capital changes or other cash adjustments; and
- Income taxes will be levied at the same effective tax rate as in 2010.

Any FCFF generated in any year will first be used to pay that year's after-tax interest expense due, and the remainder will be used to pay down as much of the outstanding debt as possible at the year end. (There is no prepayment penalty on the debt.) If there is still any FCFE remaining in any year, it will be paid out to JLR as a cash dividend.

JLR will sell 100% of its Shoppers shares at the end of 2014 such that the buyer will pay cash for the whole business, out of which JLR will repay any debt balance still outstanding and then keep any remaining cash as a payment for the shares being sold. JLR expects to be able to sell the whole business (i.e. before any debt repayment) at the end of 2014 for an amount equal to 6 times the 2015 forecasted EBITDA.

Suppose all cash flows occur at respective year ends, and all discount and growth rates are effective annual rates.

Calculate the internal rate of return (IRR) of JLR's equity investment in Shoppers' shares.

PROBLEM 6.2

Today is December 31, 2012. You are buying out Americana Inc, which currently has no cash at hand and $104 MM of bonds outstanding.

The company's EBITDA for the year just ended is $228 MM, which is expected to grow at annual rate of 3% indefinitely. The annual amortization equals the capital expenditures, which are forecasted to be $33 MM annually over the next seven years. The company faces a corporate tax rate of 35%. Assume that there are no working capital changes or other cash adjustments.

You expect to sell the company on December 31, 2018, for the median forward EV to EBITDA multiple observed for the following set of comparable companies.

Company	EV	2013 EBITDA
Comp A	7,781	1,151
Comp B	9,333	1,706
Comp C	8,047	1,409

Under the buyout terms, you will pay off all of the current debt and take on the following pieces of new debt on the date of the buyout to complete the acquisition:

- **TLA**: new balance of 2.5X EBITDA, interest rate of 7%, repayable in five equal annual instalments over the next five years
- **High-yield bonds (HYB)**: new balance of 1X EBITDA, interest rate of 9%, interest payable annually, the entire principal balance repayable at the end of the six-year term
- **PIK bonds**: Mezzanine debt of a face value of 0.5X EBITDA, currently yielding 13% to maturity (which is in seven years' time)

You will also fund the financing fees of $8 MM, investment banking fees of $4 MM, and legal and other fees of $2 MM.

Calculate the maximum value you are willing to offer for the overall target company, including the debt if you require a 20% return on this investment.

Integrated Case Study

HALF & FULL INC

© Adeel Mahmood, 2012

HALF & FULL
A Venture Capital and LBO Case Study

In December of 2010, Ms. Jennifer Half was walking her dog along the Lake Ontario shoreline, wondering what to do with her company, Half & Full, Inc. ("Half & Full"). As the co-founder and CEO of Half & Full, she felt she had built a successful business, handling many challenges over the past six years. Now, faced with the decision of whether to continue running the business or sell the company outright, she knew a poor decision might limit the future success of Half & Full.

HISTORY

Half had always enjoyed designing clothing. After graduating from McMaster in 2004, she decided to go into business with her best friend from school, Ms. Jane Full. They pulled together all the money they had and formed Half & Full, an apparel company for women, in January 2005 (the beginning of Year 1). Half contributed $30,000 and Full contributed $20,000. They were the only two founders and each "bought" founder stock at $0.01/share. As such, the initial capitalization and ownership of the Company was as follows:

Shareholders	Shares	Price	Capital Contributed
Jennifer Half	3,000,000	$0.01	$30,000
Jane Full	2,000,000	$0.01	$20,000
Total	**5,000,000**		**$50,000**

Half & Full quickly became a success. The Company's first design, an evening gown decorated with Mac the Marauder, was well received by local retailers. Working at a feverish pace, the two women sewed these first dresses themselves and shipped their first order by the end of January.

QUESTION 1

Additional orders were received soon thereafter. Exhausted after delivering the first order, Jennifer and Jane were horrified to realize that they were already nearly out of money – the fabric had cost over $30,000 and to keep up with demand they needed to buy high-powered cutting and sewing machines which would cost $80,000. Not expecting payment on the dresses for 90 days, they became concerned.

Both Jennifer and Jane were personally out of money. They went to a few local banks, but none would lend money to a company that was only a few months old. Unsure of what to do, they were relieved to get a call from Half's uncle, John Half. Uncle John offered to help by investing $150,000 in the Company. Both Jennifer and Jane knew they needed the money but were uncertain as to how much stock to issue to Uncle John in return.

Jennifer reasoned that since her uncle was willing to invest three times the amount of money as the two founders just a few months after inception, he ought to get three times as much stock as the two founders: 15,000,000 shares. Jane wanted to issue him considerably less stock since Uncle John was not a founder and was not going to work at the Company; she proposed 1,000,000 shares.

Ultimately, they agreed to offer Uncle John 3,000,000 common shares for his $150,000 ($0.05/share). He accepted and the investment closed in June 2005 (midway through Year 1).

Required:

(1A) What are the pre- and post-money valuations of the Company based on the $0.05 share price?

(1B) What percentage of the Company does Uncle John own?

QUESTION 2

During the rest of the first year of operations Half & Full continued to achieve major success. The popularity of the Company's first design led to requests from various retailers for new designs and, subsequently, many new orders. As the orders began to build up, Jennifer and Jane recognized that they would need to lease additional space, hire new employees and buy equipment. After putting pencil to paper, they decided they would need $500,000 to fund operations for Year 2 (2006).

Jennifer and Jane knew that they had an opportunity to grow the business rapidly if they could just raise the $500,000. Knowing that investors would want to see a well thought out business plan, Jennifer and Jane developed a set of financial projections based on internal forecasts and cross-checked them with publicly available data from other small apparel companies. The team projected $5.0 million of net income in Year 7 (2011), and they believed a reasonable projection for equity value at the end of Year 6 (a five year holding period from an investment close date of December 2005) would be 14x Year 7 net income.

Uncle John was pleased with the Company's progress but had no more money to invest. There were, fortunately, two other funding alternatives: First, Burlington Venture Partners, a venture capital firm investing in consumer and low-tech businesses, had contacted the founders. This venture firm was headquartered in Burlington, Ontario, and had a successful track record of investing in both early-stage and later-stage deals.

Also, the two women had recently received a call from an enthusiastic customer who was one of a group of five wealthy, retired, ex-consumer-products-and-apparel executives who invested as "angels" in start-up companies that they deemed promising. These angels enjoyed working with start-ups and had lots of relevant experience in the garment industry.

After meeting with the angel investors, Jennifer and Jane were leaning towards accepting the angel-funding alternative. The angels seemed to understand the apparel business and had some great ideas how to improve and grow Half & Full. The angels thought Jennifer and Jane were talented and energetic, and the angels thought that the financial projections were reasonable.

Jennifer and Jane understood that angels generally require a 70% internal rate of return on their investments. In anticipation of their next meeting the two women decided to model the impact on the Company's capitalization of raising $500,000 from the angels in December 2005.

Required:

(2A)   What percent of the Company would the angels have to purchase in this financing round to meet the required rate of return (assuming that no additional capital is raised by Half & Full and a five-year hold period for the angels)?

(2B) How many shares would be purchased and what would be the price/share? (Please round the price/share to the nearest cent.)

(2C) What would be the resulting pre- and post-money valuations?

QUESTION 3

The second meeting with the angels went even better than the first, and Jennifer and Jane invited the angels to invest on the terms calculated above. The angels, however, had one major concern: the deal did not meet their hurdle rate. The angels explained that in order for the Company to achieve its financial projections, the Company was almost certainly going to have to raise an additional $2,500,000 at the end of Year 2, thereby diluting the angels' ownership position. Such a large amount of money would most likely come from a venture capital firm.

Unlike Jennifer and Jane's earlier calculation, the angels wanted a 70% IRR after taking into account this anticipated dilution. Jennifer and Jane quickly revised their calculation to understand the impact of these new terms on the Company's capitalization.

Required:

(3A)   Assuming that the venture capital firm requires a 40% IRR on its investment (four-year hold) and that both investor groups anticipate the same valuation at the end of Year 6 as suggested above, what percent of the Company will the venture capital firm need to buy?

(3B)   What percent of the Company will the angels need to buy?

(3C)   How many shares will be sold in each round and at what price?

(3D)   What will the pre- and post-money valuations be at the time of each investment?

(3E)   Assuming Jennifer and Jane go through with the angel investment, calculate the post-closing capitalization table.

QUESTION 4

Despite the less attractive terms, Jennifer and Jane still thought that their best course of action was to work with the angels, and the angels made a $500,000 investment in December 2005. Jennifer and Jane were initially able to grow their Company as they had hoped. They moved into larger offices, hired additional staff, expanded the number of designs they offered and increased the number of retailers they serviced. However, cash remained tight given how quickly Half & Full was growing and the resulting working capital needs of the business. Throughout 2006 (Year 2), as the company recorded success after success, Burlington Venture Partners stayed in touch with Jennifer and Jane, hoping that the Company might once again seek to raise outside capital.

In August 2006, Half & Full secured Clothes "R" Us, a major American retailer, as their first major national reseller. This was their big break! Jennifer and Jane were at first delighted, but after reviewing the proposed contract, they concluded that Half & Full did not have the resources required to adequately support this new, large customer. They estimated that the Company would need $3.0 million to meet its obligations under the contract. Once again, Jennifer and Jane would have to seek outside capital. They consulted their angel investors who advised that now was the right time to raise venture capital from an institutional investor.

After preliminary due diligence focused on the quality of the founding team, the market potential of the business, and the major trends and risk factors in women's apparel, Burlington Venture Partners expressed an interest in investing but thought the Company might need significantly more than $3.0 million to achieve its milestones. Burlington submitted a list of additional questions to Jennifer and Jane, in order to open a dialogue and resolve some of Burlington's outstanding diligence items.

Jennifer and Jane were inclined to simply work with Burlington and conclude an investment deal quickly. However, the angels advised that it would be to the advantage of Half & Full to seek competitive offers from other venture capital firms. The angels provided several introductions and after numerous presentations to the VC firms, Jennifer and Jane received two firm investment proposals (known as "term sheets") – one from Burlington Venture Partners and one from DeGroote Venture Capital.

The terms under which Burlington and DeGroote proposed to invest, however, were a bit more complicated than the relatively simple terms that had been acceptable to Uncle John and the angels. As is customary in venture capital deals, both firms proposed to purchase Series A convertible preferred stock. "Series A" meant it was the first series of preferred stock to be sold by Half & Full. As preferred stock, it would have a senior claim to all of the assets of Half & Full and it would also contain a number of features that are typical of a preferred security.

Moreover, the investment terms proposed by Burlington were considerably different than the terms proposed by DeGroote. For example, Burlington was offering to pay $3.00 per share, while DeGroote was offering to pay $3.75. The term sheets from the VC firms are attached as Exhibits I and II.

Required:

(**4A**) Evaluate the term sheet offers proposed by Burlington and DeGroote on both a quantitative and qualitative basis, including such comparisons as the:
- Proposed pre- and post-money valuations;
- Dilution experienced by existing shareholders from the financing;
- Most significant terms proposed; and
- Financial scenarios that might make one term sheet more favorable.

(**4B**) Which term sheet do you think Half and Full should accept?

Notes:

1. **Full-ratchet** anti-dilution provisions operate by reducing the conversion price of previously issued preferred shares to match the conversion price of new shares in the dilutive issuance. In this case, if Half & Full sells Series B stock at less than the conversion price of the Series A, then the conversion price of the Series A would be reset to the conversion price of the Series B.

2. A series of preferred stock has a **"senior" liquidation preference** when it is entitled to receive its liquidation preference before another series of preferred stock. The amount of liquidation preference that a given series of preferred stock has is usually equal to the amount paid for the stock. However, in certain financings (as above), new investors may require that their liquidation preference amount be equal to more than the amount they originally invested (also referred to as a "multiple" liquidation preference). For example, if the Series B is purchased for $30 million and has a senior liquidation preference equal to two times the purchase price, then the Series B investors will receive the first $60 million on any sale of the company before the Series A or common stockholders receive any amounts.

QUESTION 5

Half & Full chose to accept Burlington's term sheet, and the investment was completed in December 2006. Soon thereafter, Jane Full announced that she would leave the Company in mid-2007 to pursue an MBA in Toronto. The Board of Directors vested all of her stock.

Realizing the need for additional professional management and heeding the Board's suggestion to strengthen the management team, Jennifer hired a VP of Finance and a Chief Operating Officer (COO). The COO was interested in Half & Full because of the challenges, excitement and potential financial upside and wanted to participate in the upside potential of the Company through equity incentives. The Board granted Quarter and the VP of Finance significant option packages from the option pool established in conjunction with Burlington's financing.

However, despite the more experienced management team, and much to the chagrin of the partners at Burlington, several serious challenges arose at Half & Full within the first six months after their investment closed: a large customer who owed the company a significant amount of money asked for a six month payment moratorium; a supply contract with a second major national reseller (key to the Company's growth plans) was awarded to a competitor; and the VP of Finance reported that the distribution expansion project required more capital than originally budgeted. Combined, these factors would lead to a major cash shortfall by the first half of 2008.

As Jennifer and her team assessed the increasingly challenging situation, they realized additional funding was needed to overcome the looming cash crunch and get the Company 'back on track'. The managers saw two main alternatives: raise an additional $2.0 million by selling Series B preferred stock or seek a bank line of credit (most likely no more than $1,250,000). After some preliminary discussions, it was clear that all VCs would insist on harsher terms and a much lower company valuation when pricing the Series B round (a so-called "down round"). Similarly, all lenders would insist that the bank line contain onerous covenants requiring a significant reduction in operating expenses immediately. It was an ugly set of choices.

After discussing each alternative, management and the Board of Directors decided to raise $2.0 million in venture capital. The Board of Directors was concerned that the bank loan would not be sufficient to cover the full funding need, leaving the company in the position of raising yet another round of capital on disadvantageous terms. Additionally, the Board noted that the Company had some key decisions on the horizon, and the bank's financial covenants might restrict the strategy or operations of the business more so than additional venture money, since venture investors would likely have a higher risk tolerance and be more focused on growth potential. Jennifer approached Burlington Ventures, as Burlington's knowledge of the Company, its deep pockets, and its desire to protect its initial investment made Burlington the most logical source of additional equity capital. At Burlington's Monday meeting, the deal team shared with their partners the disappointing news regarding Half & Full's need for additional capital. After discussing the team's recommendation, the partners authorized the negotiation of a term sheet to purchase $2.0 million of Series B preferred stock from Half & Full.

In order to finalize the investment, the Burlington team worked with Jennifer to revise the Company's projections. After detailed analysis, they projected 2010 (Year 6) net income would be $4.0 million and projected 2011 (Year 7) net income would be $5.0 million. In determining the valuation and associated conversion price for the new Series B convertible preferred shares, Burlington and the Company negotiated and agreed to the following terms and conditions:

- $2 million cash investment (with the transaction to close at year-end 2007 – Year 3);
- $12.0 million pre-money valuation for the investment (as Burlington was targeting an IRR of just over 60% on the new investment assuming a 3-year holding period and an exit value of 12 times Year 7 net income);
- Exercise of the full-ratchet provision on the previous $3.5 million Series A investment;
- 3.0x senior liquidation preference on the new Series B investment (assuming that Series B does not receive dividends); and
- An additional seat on the Board of Directors.

Required:

(5A)   Given the above parameters, calculate a new capitalization table.

(5B)   What percent ownership will Burlington receive from the new investment?

(5C)   What percent total ownership will Burlington hold after the new investment and exercise of the full-ratchet? Please calculate the resulting ownership structure on a fully-diluted basis (treat all options as exercised and outstanding at a zero strike price).

QUESTION 6

In the ensuing months and years, the Company overcame the cash crunch and experienced significant success. Half & Full aggressively expanded its international distribution infrastructure and built a few corporate-owned retail locations in the U.S. in high end shopping areas. The company showed the potential of becoming the next DKNY or Calvin Klein.

Unexpectedly, in November 2010, two interested parties approached Half and proposed strategic transactions. Clothes "R" Us expressed interest in making a strategic investment and a private equity investment firm named **Buyouts V** asked Half if she would consider selling the entire Company in an all-cash transaction. Buyouts V had extensive experience in the apparel industry and had acquired several apparel companies over the years.

Jennifer knew that Uncle John and the angel investors liked the idea of "cashing out" via an IPO or sale of the Company; some wanted to reinvest their profits into other early stage deals while others simply wanted to lock in a profit. Burlington Venture Partners, impressed with Jennifer's handling of the previous challenges, said the decision was up to her. Jennifer wasn't sure what she wanted herself. As she walked along the lake, she contemplated her options.

Ultimately in early December 2010, Jennifer decided that an all-cash sale to Buyouts V could be very attractive. She expected that Buyouts V would place a high enterprise value on the firm and the Company had no debt. Jennifer was also beginning to worry that her management team might not be strong enough to run a much larger company, and prudence dictated that she get the best price she could now for the shareholders. Half called Buyouts V and told them she was open to considering an offer and would like them to present their offer at next week's Board meeting.

The managers of Buyouts V (known as the "General Partners") strive to deliver an attractive rate of return to the investors in Buyouts V (known as "Limited Partners"). Buyout V's Limited Partners have traditionally required a 20% net IRR (i.e., after carried interest and assuming a 2% annual management fees over a 5-year investment horizon). Under the terms of the Buyouts V Partnership Agreement, the General Partners are entitled to a "carried interest" of 20% of the profits, or capital gain.

Required:

(6A) Given the target net return of 20% to the Limited Partners, what "deal-level" multiple of investment and IRR should Buyouts V target for the acquisition of Half and Full?

(6B) What do you think will be the consequences if this investment does not meet Buyouts V's objective of achieving a 20% net return to its Limited Partners?

QUESTION 7

Buyouts V wants to structure the transaction as a traditional LBO in order to maximize its return on equity, while maintaining reasonable interest coverage ratios. Buyouts V expects to finance the transaction with 2.0x 2011 EBITDA of senior debt and 1.5x 2011 EBITDA of subordinated debt. The remaining cash consideration will be financed with equity. The senior debt and subordinated debt carry fixed annual interest rates of 5.5% and 10%, respectively.

Buyouts V is excited about this investment but needs to make sure the deal meets the Fund's designated investment hurdle rate. After several meetings with Half's management team and some industry due diligence, Buyouts V develops the following assumptions:

- 2010 EBITDA of $6.4 million;
- 12.5% annual EBITDA growth;
- Depreciation to equal one-quarter of EBITDA;
- Capital expenditures in a year to equal the depreciation for the year;
- Corporate tax rate of 35%;
- Working capital and other cash adjustments to equal zero;
- A minimum cash balance of $2.0 million to remain on the Company's balance sheet at all times following the acquisition;
- Interest income of 2% annually will be earned on all cash on the balance sheet;
- Buyouts V to purchase the company without any cash on the balance sheet and retain all cash on the balance sheet, if any, at the time of sale;
- All remaining free cash flow used to repay senior debt ONLY (i.e., no repayment of subordinated debt until maturity), with any free cash flow remaining after the repayment of senior debt accumulating to cash on hand;
- Subordinated debt matures in 10 years and does not require any principal amortization until Year 10 (i.e., no free cash flow is required to pay down subordinated debt prior to Year 10 although cash interest payments are made in each year);
- Employees of the company granted 8% of the ownership in Half & Full in the form of options with a zero strike price, with all options "vesting" upon a change of control;
- Sale of the company in December 2015 (five years after the LBO) for an EV of 6.0 times forward EBITDA;
- No financing costs or transaction fees; and
- Target deal-level IRR of 25%.

Required:

(7A) The next step for Buyouts V is to develop a financial model based on the assumptions above. What is the highest price that Buyouts V should be willing to pay for the company (debt plus equity)?

QUESTION 8

The assumptions above represented Buyouts V's best estimate of the Company's performance given its current understanding of the Company and the apparel industry; however, the partners recognized that circumstances can and do change over the course of a multi-year investment. As such, Buyouts V wanted to analyze how sensitive its returns were to changes in EBITDA growth rate, exit multiple, and beginning financial leverage.

Required:

(8A) Holding the purchase price calculated in Question **7A** constant, calculate Buyout 5's multiple of investment and IRR given each of the following changes independently:
- EBITDA growth of 7.5%
- EBITDA growth of 17.5%
- Exit multiple of 5.0x
- Exit multiple of 7.0x
- 2.5x senior debt and 2.0x subordinated debt
- 1.5x senior debt and 1.0x subordinated debt

(8B) Based on the ranges used in Question **8A**, to which variable is the IRR the most sensitive? How might Buyouts V use this knowledge to its benefit?

QUESTION 9

Buyouts V presented its offer to the Company's Board on Monday morning. After they left, a spirited discussion took place regarding the best strategy for the Company to follow. A strong consensus emerged that it would be attractive to sell at a price of $41.5 million. If Buyouts V was unwilling to pay that much, then the Company could seek other bidders, work out a strategic partnership with Clothes"R"Us, or simply keep marching towards an IPO. Half called Buyouts V after the Board meeting and told them they had until noon the next day to decide whether to raise their offer.

Half got the good news by voicemail on her way to work early Tuesday morning. While waiting in line to order her usual morning coffee, Half, in a moment of indulgence, decided to order a double and to actually sit in the coffee shop and enjoy drinking it. Already she was beginning to think about taking a vacation – her first in many years. "Should I visit the South Pacific or the Caribbean?" Half mused, as she savored the fresh flavor of her coffee.

Required:

Assume the buyout closed on December 31, 2010, at a purchase price of $41.5 million for the total firm (including debt and equity).

(9A)   Calculate, on a pre-tax basis, the aggregate dollar exit proceeds, the aggregate dollar profit, the multiple of investment, and the IRR for each stockholder from the sale. Assume a six-year holding period for Half and Full, a five and a half-year holding period for Uncle John, a five-year holding period for the angel investment, and a four-year holding period for Burlington's initial investment and a three-year holding period for Burlington's second investment.

Assume the buyout will be considered a "liquidation event" under the terms of the Preferred Stock. Thus, Burlington must choose between receiving a liquidation preference or converting each of its Series A and Series B Preferred shares. Assume all available options are issued and outstanding at the time of the acquisition at a zero strike price.

(9B)   Compare and discuss the aggregate dollar profits, multiple of investment and IRR for each shareholder.

QUESTION 10

Jennifer Half's involvement with Half & Full ended soon after selling the company. Both Half and Buyouts V believed that the company was ready for more experienced management as its operations became more complex. Buyouts V recruited several managers from apparel designers and retailers (including Clothes "R" Us). Half agreed to remain with the company for a brief time post-LBO to assist with the management transition before enrolling full-time in DeGroote's MBA program. While she enjoyed the thrills of pre-term and core classes, her company continued under the ownership of Buyouts V.

After Buyouts V completed its LBO of Half & Full, the business performed according to plan. At the time of the LBO, lenders were relatively risk averse and unwilling to support a total leverage multiple above 3.5x for an apparel business of Half & Full's size. However, independent of the company's operating performance, the risk appetite of creditors increased as capital markets conditions changed. After owning S&H for three years, Buyouts V was presented with an opportunity to "recapitalize" Half and Full at the end of 2013. In this context, recapitalize means to change the capital structure by borrowing additional funds to finance a dividend to equity owners. (This is commonly called a leveraged recap or a dividend recap.)

On December 31, 2013, Half & Full borrowed additional funds to increase borrowing of senior debt to 2.5x 2013 EBITDA and subordinated debt to 2.0x 2013 EBITDA, both at the same interest rates as before. On the same date, the Company declared a cash dividend to its shareholders equal to the amount of the total proceeds from incremental borrowing.

Two years later (on December 31, 2015), Buyouts V sold the Company to Clothes "R" Us for 6.0x forward EBITDA.

Required:

(10A) Calculate, on a pre-tax basis, the aggregate dollar exit proceeds, the aggregate dollar profit, the multiple of investment, and the IRR for Buyouts V. (Assume the actual operating results are the same as the original operating projections. Ignore any tax implications of the 2013 recapitalization and distributions.)

(10B) How do the multiple of investment and IRR compare with the original projections?

(10C) LBO financial returns can result from several sources. For example, revenue growth, improvement in operating margins, additional leverage, and an expansion of the exit multiple would all produce incremental financial returns. What were the major drivers of financial return for this LBO transaction? Based on what you generally know about the apparel industry, what types of business trends could underlie these drivers?

EXHIBIT I
BURLINGTON VENTURE PARTNERS LLC
MEMORANDUM OF TERMS
FOR THE PROPOSED SERIES A PREFERRED STOCK
FINANCING OF HALF & FULL, INC

OFFERING TERMS

Issuer:	Half & Full, Inc (the "Company")
Securities to Be Issued:	Series A Preferred Stock (the "Preferred")
Anticipated Closing Date:	On or before December 31, 2006
Aggregate Proceeds:	$3.5 million
Price:	$3.00 per share
Number of Shares to Be Issued:	1,166,666 shares of the Preferred
Option Pool:	The option pool available for future issuance will consist of 20% of the Company on a fully-diluted basis (post-financing)
Post-Closing Capitalization Table:	[TO BE DETERMINED BY STUDENTS]

TERMS OF SERIES A PREFERRED STOCK

Dividends

The holders of the Preferred shall be entitled to receive 10% cumulative cash dividends in preference to any dividends on common stock (the "Common"), if declared by the Board of Directors. The dividend will not compound. No dividend shall be paid on the Common in any year until all current and accrued dividends on the Preferred have been paid.

Liquidation Preference

In the event of a Liquidation, the holders of the Preferred shall be entitled to receive, in preference to the holders of the Common, an amount equal to (i) the purchase price per share of Preferred, plus (ii) all accrued but unpaid dividends.

A Liquidation is defined as a merger, reorganization, or other transaction in which control of the Company is transferred.

Conversion

Each holder of the Preferred shall have the right to convert his or her shares of Preferred at any time, at the option of the holder, into shares of Common The conversion rate shall initially be 1:1, and shall be subject to antidilution adjustments, as provided below.

Antidilution Adjustments

The price of the Preferred shall be subject to adjustment, on a full-ratchet basis, to prevent dilution in the event that the Company issues additional shares (excluding options issued under the Company's option plan) at a purchase price per share less than the current price of the Preferred.

Voting Rights

The holders of each share of Preferred shall have the right to a number of votes equal to the number of shares of Common issuable upon the conversion of the Preferred.

Representations and Warranties

Standard representations and warranties are provided by the Company.

Board of Directors

The Board shall consist of a total of five (5) members. The holders of a majority of the Preferred shall be entitled to elect two (2) representatives on the Board of Directors. One (1) outside member shall be mutually agreed to among the holders of a majority of the Preferred and the Common. The remaining two (2) members shall be from the Company's management team.

Right of First Refusal

Until the completion of an Initial Public Offering, the Preferred will have a pro rata right to participate in subsequent equity financings of the Company (subject to customary exclusions).

Vesting of Common Stock and Options

Common and options shall vest as follows: after 12 months of employment, 25%; the remainder will vest monthly over the next three years.

Legal Fees and Expenses

The Company shall pay the reasonable fees and expenses of a single counsel to the investors.

EXHIBIT II

OFFERING TERMS

Issuer:	Half & Full, Inc (the "Company")
Securities to Be Issued:	Series A Preferred Stock (the "Preferred")
Anticipated Closing Date:	On or before December 31, 2006
Aggregate Proceeds:	$2.75 million
Price:	$3.75 per share
Number of Shares to Be Issued:	733,333 shares of the Preferred
Option Pool:	The option pool available for future issuance will consist of 20% of the Company on a fully-diluted basis (post-financing)
Post-Closing Capitalization Table:	[TO BE DETERMINED BY STUDENTS]

TERMS OF SERIES A PREFERRED STOCK

Dividends

The holders of the Preferred shall be entitled to receive 10% cumulative dividends in preference to any dividends on common stock (the "Common"), if declared by the Board of Directors. The dividend will not compound. No dividend shall be paid on the Common in any year until all current and accrued dividends on the Preferred have been paid.

Liquidation Preference

In the event of a Liquidation, the holders of the Preferred shall be entitled to receive, in preference to the holders of the Common, an amount equal to (i) two (2.0) times the purchase price per share of Preferred, plus (ii) two (2.0) times all accrued but unpaid dividends.

Liquidation is defined as a merger, reorganization, or other transaction in which control of the Company is transferred.

Conversion

Each holder of the Preferred shall have the right to convert his or her shares of Preferred at any time, at the option of the holder, into shares of Common The conversion rate shall initially be 1:1, and shall be subject to antidilution adjustments, as provided below.

Antidilution Adjustments

The price of the Preferred shall be subject to adjustment, on a full-ratchet basis, to prevent dilution in the event that the Company issues additional shares (excluding options issued under the Company's option plan) at a purchase price per share less than the current price of the Preferred.

Voting Rights

The holders of each share of Preferred shall have the right to a number of votes equal to the number of shares of Common issuable upon the conversion of the Preferred.

Representations and Warranties

Standard representations and warranties are provided by the Company.

Board of Directors

The Board shall consist of a total of five (5) members. The holders of a majority of the Preferred shall be entitled to elect three (3) representatives on the Board of Directors. One (1) outside member shall be mutually agreed to among the holders of a majority of the Preferred and the Common. The remaining one (1) member shall be from the Company's management team.

Right of First Refusal

Until the completion of an Initial Public Offering, the Preferred will have a pro rata right to participate in subsequent equity financings of the Company (subject to customary exclusions).

Vesting of Common Stock and Options

Common and options shall vest as follows: after 12 months of employment, 25%; the remainder will vest monthly over the next three years.

Legal Fees and Expenses

The Company shall pay the reasonable fees and expenses of a single counsel to the investors.

9-805-019
REV: DECEMBER 1, 2004

MICHAEL J. ROBERTS

LAUREN BARLEY

How Venture Capitalists Evaluate Potential Venture Opportunities

We interviewed four venture capitalists from leading Silicon Valley firms to learn about the frameworks they use in evaluating potential venture opportunities. (See **Exhibit 1** for background information on these venture capital firms.) All four were interviewed individually and were asked similar questions, such as "How do you evaluate potential venture opportunities?" "How do you evaluate the venture's prospective business model?" "What due diligence do you conduct?" "What is the process through which funding decisions are made?" "What financial analyses do you perform?" "What role does risk play in your evaluation?" and "How do you think about a potential exit route?" The following are excerpts from these interviews.

Russell Siegelman: Partner, Kleiner Perkins Caufield & Byers (KPCB)

Russ Siegelman joined KPCB in 1996 after seven years with Microsoft Corporation, where he helped found and launch Microsoft Network (MSN). Before working at Microsoft, he wrote artificial intelligence software. Siegelman invests in software, electronic commerce, Web services, telecommunications, and media and sits on the boards of Vertical Networks, Lilliputian Systems, Mobilygen, Quorum Systems, Digital Chocolate, and Vividence. He is one of the managing partners of the KPCB XI Fund, which closed in February 2004. Siegelman earned his B.S. from the Massachusetts Institute of Technology in physics in 1984 and an MBA from Harvard Business School in 1989.

How Do You Evaluate Potential Venture Opportunities?

"We have a generally understood set of things we look for when we evaluate an investment opportunity. The most important requirement is a large market opportunity in a fast-growing sector. Explosive growth makes it difficult for somebody to catch up or incumbents to respond. We like a company to have a $100 million to $300 million revenue stream within five years. This means that the market potential has to be at least $500 million—or more, eventually—and the company needs to achieve at least a 25% market share.

"The second factor involves a competitive edge that is long lasting. It could be a network effect like eBay or an operating system lock-in like Microsoft, but those are few and far between. It is usually an engineering challenge that is tough enough to build an edge, resulting in several years lead or longer, if we're lucky. We look for a tough problem that hasn't been solved before. The solution can't be so straightforward that someone can look at the blackboard and say, 'I know how to do it.' We tend to avoid 'scientific breakthroughs'—we're not great at evaluating or managing science projects. We know how to take technology, commercialize it, and turn it into a viable business.

"We are a little schizophrenic on patents. Personally, I don't care much about patents; they are a nice-to-have but not a requirement. Only a couple of our companies hold patents that are worth much. Once a technology is patented, it's out there and people figure out a way to get around it. However, we do conduct patent searches to make sure no one is blocking us. We have several companies that would rather keep their intellectual property a trade secret. Not everyone agrees with that here; we have some partners who are fond of big patent portfolios.

"The third thing is team. There are lots of aspects to the team. We look for a strong technical founder—if it is a tough, technical problem—and a sales-oriented entrepreneur. The founder is the anchor, more than just an idea person, who understands the whole thrust behind the technology and the industry dynamic around it. The entrepreneur drives the other parts of the business and sells the vision to investors and to other early-stage participants such as full-time employees, partners, and potential customers. We look for engineering vision and execution, sales, and entrepreneurship in a team. Typically, it's at least two people; sometimes it's three.

"In the early stages, I tend to invest behind an entrepreneur, not behind a professional manager as the CEO. Often, the person who can professionally manage as a CEO in the later stages of a company is not as effective in the earlier stages. It requires a different skill set. Entrepreneurs have to have a clear sense of the opportunity and how to build the business. That is why we're willing to bet on them and what we're paying them for. But, the best ones are willing to reexamine their assumptions and are willing to veer left or right or pivot all the way around when the data suggests they're headed in the wrong direction. They amble around until they find something good. The bad ones typically get overcommitted or wed to a particular idea. By the way, professional managers, who join the company later on, are the reverse. Once they're in and there's a proven business model, we want them to be committed and not to be exploring other business models.

"So overall it's a funny mix. When we review an investment opportunity, entrepreneurs have to have a pretty good story to tell about what they want to do. I think it helps to be cocky, there's no doubt about it. You can be too cocky, sometimes we're a little bit mindful of that . . . but if you're not cocky enough, you're not going to be successful in selling your idea."

How Do You Evaluate the Venture's Prospective Business Model?

"To oversimplify, I'd say there are two broad kinds of investment opportunities. In the first bucket, the market or product is somewhat understood. The company is doing a better execution or a better version of an existing product or service—with a twist—in a proven market. We are investing behind a business model that we are fairly sure we understand. We expect the business plan to reflect the anticipated business model and that it's credible—it meets the 'smell test.'

"Then, there are completely new markets or business models where we *think* we may know the bets we're making, but in truth we have no clue. Friendster's a good, recent example: explosive growth, potential network effects, and an unclear business model. We invested in it over six months ago. The business model is either advertising based or pay-for-contact, but we haven't tried either yet. We identified the business model as a big risk when we invested. However, we thought Friendster had enough growth potential, and there were enough 'game-changing' aspects to it that we were willing to make the bet. When we invested in Amazon, it was clearly new. However, there was an early proof point because it was already selling books worth a few million dollars per quarter on the Internet. It was too early to tell if it could maintain significant margins or build a billion-dollar revenue company. But we knew something good was happening.

"Here's a case that didn't work. We invested in a company that conducted a barter-type swap meet, online. It seemed like an interesting idea, a twist on eBay with potentially a different approach to the market. It didn't work. To this day, I'm not sure if it was bad execution or a wrongheaded plan. We certainly have invested behind new ideas that didn't work.

"Timing is critical to successful venture capital investing, but it is not well understood. The timing of the investment and the rate the money goes in make the difference in the financial return. There are some companies where we invested too early. A later investor—perhaps one who entered after the first or second investment round—made the high returns. We've also invested too late: companies that were good companies, but they missed the window and competitors beat them to the punch. Our money was not as efficient as the money that was invested earlier in the sector. But it's hard to fine-tune; it's a gut thing."

What Due Diligence Do You Conduct?

"Technical due diligence is a big part of the data we consider when engineering innovation is involved. One of our companies is trying to solve a really difficult engineering problem, one of the hardest engineering problems I've seen in my eight years here. We did a lot of technical due diligence on this opportunity. We had probably six meetings where professors from Berkeley and consultants we hired pored over every aspect of the technology. We invested partly because the smart guys said it couldn't be done; it was really too hard to do. But after they looked at it, they said, 'These guys have made good progress; they're asking all the right questions; they have a reasonable, potential solution; and, if they can do it, it's the only way because all the other avenues we know about are dead ends.'

"Another part of due diligence involves customers. With most of the opportunities we seriously pursue, the market data is unclear because the company has no customers and revenue. Frequently, we brief potential customers about the product concept, but often they haven't met the company. Sometimes, they've met the company, but there's no product. Sometimes, they've met the company but not under nondisclosure agreement, so they don't have the full story. We have to filter all that. We have to ferret out what the customers' real needs are and their willingness to pay. But it's all sketchy and really hard to do. Occasionally, the companies have customers and revenue, so it's easier to evaluate. Then the question becomes do we want to pay up for that in the valuation. It's typically not in our sweet zone if the venture already has customers and a lot of revenue. But sometimes we do these 'speed ups'—like Amazon—and sometimes they are very successful.

"Then there's a third kind of due diligence, the industry due diligence. There, we probe industry experts about the idea, the team, the market, and the market need. They are not the customers per se but either technical or business experts in our network or people we think might have an opinion on a proposed investment.

"The fourth kind of due diligence is on the entrepreneur and team. We call their references and blind references. We spend a lot of time with them. We try to triangulate on how they've executed, are they honest, and are they people we want to work with.

"Some projects speak to a lot of due diligence—like the company with the difficult engineering challenge. With Friendster, what due diligence did we have to do? It was all about the business angle, the model, and the momentum. There was no new engineering problem being solved. The big due diligence we did for Friendster was to identify the competitors with the most momentum and look at usage and membership statistics. There was some concern that Friendster might be too easy to copy. In the end, we had to decide if we wanted to get behind the model, the entrepreneur, and the team. Usually there is not a ton of data. I go with my gut on whether it is a good bet or not. The due diligence will only take you so far, and then you have to use judgment based on experience."

What Is the Process through Which Funding Decisions Are Made?

"We have particular investment hypotheses we lay out in the investment proposal. We typically list three or four key risks we want to mitigate with the money going in. Sometimes, we stage the investment. We've done this with some medical device companies. They had to build the device and show it could be used in an animal study. In one case, it was only a $3 million investment. We put in one million up front, another million to build the prototype, and the third million for the animal study. The whole idea was to mitigate risk. But often that doesn't make sense. In some cases, there are no meaningful milestones that the team can achieve with a million dollars, so you have to invest more money initially. Or sometimes, there is so much competition coming that you don't have the luxury of the 'test and go slow approach.'

"Our smallest investment is $500,000 for an angel, seed, or incubation type of investment. Typically, our first round is $3 million to $5 million with the assumption that over the course of the company our investment will be about $10 million. We have a couple of companies where we've invested $40 million or $50 million over the course of the company's life, but that is the exception.

"The average plan takes six weeks from initial meeting until we invest in it, sometimes even longer. I invested in a chip company in San Diego that took a long time. We first met the team in October and closed in the second week in March. But during the bubble years, deals got done in an hour. Even now, hot opportunities like Friendster don't take more than two to three weeks. We met Jonathan Abrams—Friendster's founder—over a weekend. That next Monday he was at Kleiner. John Doerr and I went to the company on Tuesday and spent more time on it during the week. The following Monday, Jonathan came in for a partner meeting. We closed the following Sunday. That opportunity was going to get taken away by someone; we couldn't wait."

What Financial Analyses Do You Perform?

"We don't focus on value chain or margin analysis typically. If it's a new market or a twist on an existing product, it's not always clear how much competition there will be or how much customers are willing to pay. In some cases, I think we have some well-understood guideposts. Software should be high gross margin, but the question becomes the cost to distribute or sell. If it is an enterprise product, the company needs to sell it for $200,000 at a minimum, or it can't afford a direct sales force. The margin analysis is implicit in that logic. If the price is lower, then the issue is around channel strategy. Usually we won't invest in an opportunity with a lower-price point product unless there's already some proven low-price channel that can efficiently distribute the product. That is not a very sophisticated margin analysis, but that's how we think about it on the software side.

"On the hardware side, we are focused on the BOM [bill of materials] and the selling price. If the BOM looks like we can get a 50% gross margin at reasonable volumes, then it's a gross margin that's reasonable. We look to see if there are well-established channels to sell that product. If it's a consumer retail product, we need to understand how much inventory to build to calculate carrying costs. I would say we do some analysis, but it's not terribly deep; we basically use rules of thumb.

"Some venture capitalists put a lot of faith in the financials that are projected; I usually put very little. Most of the plan doesn't materialize the way the entrepreneur expects. The financials are usually not even close. Sometimes they're way better; sometimes they're way worse. I look at the financials because they are a credibility test for the entrepreneur. Are they reasonable and consistent with the operational needs of the business? If the person is telling a story about low-cost distribution or premium pricing, I want to see that built into the numbers at a fine level of detail.

"Sometimes I'll think an idea is interesting initially, and then I'll get to the financial section. I'll realize the person had a couple of good ideas but no clue about how to build a business because the financials are so disconnected from the reality of the strategy or operations. I wouldn't necessarily reject the person because it could be a fabulous technical entrepreneur with no business experience. But usually, it is a warning sign that I don't have a complete entrepreneur. A good entrepreneur understands both the technical and business opportunities and how to flesh out the numbers behind it."

What Role Does Risk Play in Your Evaluation?

"I think that a risk-to-reward ratio is a good way to think about the rationale for investing in an opportunity. We are doing that calibration in the back of our minds, but no one goes to the blackboard and says this specific upside is worth this risk. It is too hard to quantify.

"I would say close to 100% of the time the original plan does not come to reality, sometimes in a good way and sometimes in a bad way. The founders didn't realize they had something completely wrong and had to overcome it. Or the opposite, we overlooked some great attribute in the original plan. So the point is, we have to view an opportunity as a multichapter novel. The business plan is the prologue or the book jacket summary because there is no real business yet. We write the contents of the book together, and that is how it works.

"We have these off-sites once a year. Three out of four years, we'll look at companies we were sorry we didn't invest in. I'm not sure how constructive it is other than to confirm that we're seeing a large percentage of the good opportunities here in the Valley. On the ones we saw but didn't invest in that were successful, we say, 'Hey, we screwed that one up.'"

How Do You Think about a Potential Exit Route?

"We want to invest in an opportunity if it is big enough to turn into a successful, sustainable, IPO-able company. Companies that are built to be sold in an acquisition do not typically excite us. That is the culture of the firm. I think it's because we have a limited number of investing partners, and our business model is to build substantial IPO-able companies.

"We may overdo it. I've had the view here that it is great to swing for the fences, but it is also okay to get a ground rule double occasionally if it's got lower risk. Or something that looks like a home run but at a minimum turns into a double is not a bad thing. But, fundamentally, the firm's appetite is for very high return and very high-risk projects. One can't argue with that approach too much since it has worked so well in the past."

Sonja Hoel: Managing Director, Menlo Ventures

Sonja Hoel joined Menlo Ventures in 1994 after working for Symantec Corporation in business development and as an analyst for TA Associates. Her focus is early-stage software, communications, and Internet investments. Hoel's recent investments and board seats are Acme Packet, iS3, MailFrontier, nCircle Network Security, and Q1 Labs. Her prior investments and board seats were AssureNet Pathways, Eloquent, F5 Networks, Priority Call, Recourse Technologies, and Vermeer Technologies. She received her B.S. in commerce from the University of Virginia and an MBA from Harvard Business School in 1993.

How Do You Evaluate Potential Venture Opportunities?

"It is all about the market. I always look at the market first. 'Market' is not how to sell a can of Coke or a car on TV. It is more strategic than that: It includes evaluating market growth, market size, competition, and customer adoption rates. If a company has a great market, it doesn't need to have a complete management team or positioning story or sizzle or PR or whatever. The corporate details can be filled in later. Some venture capitalists say they only want to invest in the very best people; they look at the team first. We funded a deal once because we really liked the CEO; he's a really great CEO. Unfortunately, the company wasn't a great company because it didn't have a large enough market.

"My favorite company is the kind of company that is doing well despite itself. It is a lot of work because we have to find the management team; we have to build. I invested in a company that has technology that looks at corporate networks to determine security system holes and vulnerabilities. The company had an interim CEO and a very good VP of engineering and CFO. But, if you asked the company or customers what the company's product did, you would get a different answer every time. However, the company had seven Fortune 100 customers willing to spend over $100,000 each on the product. We brought in a new CEO, VP of sales, and VP of marketing. We worked with the management team to position the product and develop a new user interface. We have this great company now; we've got amazing customers and a great team. We basically defined a new market space. It's a story of a company that is doing incredibly well despite some early missteps because there was a large, untapped, and growing market for its product.

"Sometimes we don't know if the market is big or small, especially in these emerging spaces. I was involved in a company called F5 Networks that did load balancing for Web sites. We invested when it had very little in cumulative sales. We thought it was going to be hot because the number of Web sites was exploding, and performance mattered to consumers. The company took off like a rocket: revenues went from $200,000 to $27 million to over $100 million. The rest is history, and it's still public. But it was an emerging market; there wasn't a market for this product the year before. This also speaks to hitting a market at the right time. We don't want to miss a market window because it takes a long time for a market to develop.

"We have a process here called 'SEMS,' or systematic emerging market selection. We do a SEMS project for every investment we make. Twice a year at our planning meeting, we talk about new markets or problems that need to be solved. We've been looking at e-mail through this process because there are a lot of unsolved problems, like spam. Every single person and every single enterprise in the world has a problem with spam, and they don't have to be educated about it. We spent a year researching every antispam company out there before we invested in one.

"When we look at markets, we ask, 'Is the Fortune 1000 the target for this company?' For the network security company, it absolutely is. Fortune 1000 companies are willing to pay hundreds of

6

thousands of dollars to solve their network security problems, so we get a pretty big market that way. We look for markets to be $500 million to $1 billion in size. When we analyze our past performance, we find that when we miss, we miss on market size. We thought the market was going to be big, but it wasn't.

"Vertical markets can be difficult. We had a company with a product to detect fraud, but it was only sold to the insurance market. Fraud in insurance is a problem, but it just wasn't a big enough market. On the other hand, we had a company called HNC Software that looked for fraud in credit cards. Fraud in the credit card market is huge, and that company went public and is still selling its product today.

"We track four things and relate them to the success of our investments: market size, the team, unique technology, and whether the product is developed at the time we invest. We found proprietary technology is important but doesn't make much of a difference as a unique differentiator for huge returns. Market size and a developed product matter most. We have much better luck if the product is in beta or shipping, although we do invest in start-ups without a developed product. Often someone comes in and says they have a great new technology, but they haven't looked at the market the technology is going to serve. Security is famous for this: we have better encryption, but who cares? It's all about solving a problem.

"In order to create a barrier, the technology has got to be hard to execute. Some companies have patents; some don't. We encourage them to have patents because it's a more litigious environment than it was 10 years ago. Regardless, the company can't have a product that is easily commoditized and that can be knocked off in a week. Enterprise software applications require man-years of building to develop the user interface and back-end connections.

"We also look at the management team. If we've got a founder who's in it for the lifestyle or unwilling to upgrade the team if necessary, we have a conversation about their willingness to hire new team members. Usually they say yes, and we need that flexibility.

"We also look at location. It is very easy to hire good people in Silicon Valley and in the Boston area. In other places, it's a lot more difficult. I invested in a company in North Carolina early in my career. It was acquired, which was a reasonable outcome for the management team, but it was difficult to get noticed because there wasn't a big technology pool there."

How Do You Evaluate the Venture's Prospective Business Model?

"You need to have a strategy for what your business model is. I get really tough on business models. If a company is selling an enterprise product, we can figure out the margins and distribution before we start. For example, if a company has a $15,000 product that is expected to be sold through a direct sales force, it's not going to work because a direct sales force is going to cost a lot more than the revenue it'll bring in. We don't focus too much on the SOHO [small office, home office] market because we think it requires a direct sale, but the price point is too low. Most of our companies either use direct sales or telesales to sell their product or service. If you can sell your product over the phone, that is fantastic. Over time, many of our companies sell through third-party channels as well."

What Due Diligence Do You Conduct?

"Customers are the most important reference. The conversation goes like this: 'If there were a product that would do this, would you buy it? What problem would it solve for you, and how important is that problem? How much would you pay for this product?' That's the big mistake a lot of entrepreneurs make. They don't talk to customers first. Maybe they have a unique technology, but it doesn't count for much if no one will buy it.

"We do the due diligence in-house, but we also use our entrepreneurs from previous investments. We have been investing in information technology for years. If we've got an opportunity that is related to a previous investment, we'll show it to the VP of engineering or CEO. Those checks are very helpful."

What Is the Process through Which Funding Decisions Are Made?

"A deal takes anywhere from a month to many months to get done. Usually from start to finish is a two- to three-month period. We're looking at a company now that was a seed deal a year and a half ago, but we wanted to wait until they had a few more customers or a few beta sites. Now they're back, and they've made a lot of progress, which is good. We can work fast if it's something that is really hot. We find the more analysis we do trying to figure out something, the weaker the deal is. If it's not clear to us, there is probably a good reason.

"We want to have $20 million to $25 million in each company. We will probably have 60 to 75 investments in Menlo IX, which is a $1.5 billion fund, so that is about right. We invest over the life of the company. With a little company, we might start off with $5 million to $8 million and put in more over time. What we've found is that if we think it's a good deal, we should invest as much money as possible."

What Financial Analyses Do You Perform?

"I look at the financials to see if they make sense. I actually look at them more for mistakes. If someone thinks they will have a 40% after-tax margin after five years, they clearly do not understand the costs of running a business. We do some forecasts and projections for our investment summaries in a really brief way. Detailed projections are usually not accurate and not that meaningful. We can guess all we want, but if we have a big, growing market and some people who can implement well, we should have significant revenues over time.

"Every August, we do this analysis about deals we turned down either because of market, management, technology, or the product wasn't developed. We almost always get it right if we turned down a deal because there wasn't a market. Where we don't always get it right is valuation. If we turn it down because of valuation, we had a 10% error rate. Of all the decisions we made because of valuation, 90% were good but 10% were bad. With market as a reason, 99% were good and only 1% were bad decisions."

What Role Does Risk Play in Your Evaluation?

"We try to reduce our risk by investing in companies that are the market share leader or are going to be the market share leader in their space. We talk to analysts, customers, or other experts in the space to identify and evaluate those companies. Companies that are market leaders typically have greater margin and a larger cushion to make mistakes, and they are usually the first ones to go public. They can also hire the best people. We've looked at thousands and thousands of companies and have evaluated what they've done right and wrong; we've developed a nose for which companies are going to be number one. Our investment processes also help us reduce risk. We've talked about our SEMS process. When we do our valuation analysis, we do comparables, and if the opportunity looks like it will return less than five times our investment, we won't do it. Our returns have to be seven to 10 times because venture capital investments are high risk."

How Do You Think about a Potential Exit Route?

"We have to think IPO [initial public offering] all the time; this company could go public. However, it has become harder for small companies to go public because of new regulations that make an acquisition a more attractive outcome. We've had a couple of liquidity events recently. Big companies didn't do their R&D [research and development] in the last four or five years because of profit pressures. I think there will be a lot of acquisitions coming because there are holes in product lines, and existing companies have access to distribution so they can take a product, insert it in their product line, and sell it."

Fred Wang: General Partner, Trinity Ventures

Fred Wang joined Trinity Ventures as a general partner in 1999 from Spectrum Equity Investors. Wang has spent over 15 years in the communications industry, working at The Boston Consulting Group with clients such as AT&T, Lucent, and Siemens as well as in operating positions in the new technologies groups at Pacific Bell and Intuit. Wang's focus at Trinity is on communications and networked systems, services, and semiconductors. He sits on seven boards of Trinity's portfolio companies. Wang received his B.S. in electrical engineering and M.S. in industrial engineering from Stanford University and an MBA from Harvard Business School in 1992.

How Do You Evaluate Potential Venture Opportunities?

"There is not a formal template, per se. There are some pretty obvious things—in no particular order for us, they are team, market opportunity, and the product/value proposition for the solution. Technology differentiation or business model differentiation is also important to sustain a competitive advantage.

"One potential point of differentiation between us and some other firms relates to how we think about the CEO. A couple of years ago, we analyzed our successful companies across multiple dimensions. The one trait of all our successful companies was that the CEO we backed at funding was still the CEO at the sale of the company or IPO. We'll switch out CEOs; we've done that and had decent outcomes, but our best outcomes are the ones where the CEO takes it to glory. Historically, we have not been as good at bringing in a CEO when a company goes sideways.

"I think our focus on the CEO has helped us eliminate one set of mistakes we might have been making. During the bubble years, we funded companies when we knew that the CEO was the wrong CEO or there wasn't a true CEO in place. We thought we'd find the right CEO down the road. We'd have the conversation with the company about getting a new CEO in place, but it was never the right time. So now, to fund a company, we need to believe that the existing CEO could bring the company to a successful outcome.

"As a result, we spend a lot of time focused on the CEO and the members of the management team: the quality of people they attract, their biases, their strong points, and their overall depth. Part of that is more experiential, and much of it's in the due diligence. We spend a lot of time in a room with the management team going through problems. What's the channel? What happens if the customer comes back and says this? What happens in product development? Hearing how they think

9

and react is very helpful. We pick up a lot of insight on how they would operate the business day to day.

"We've also done some analysis that suggests another big determinant of success is the sector; it's a sector bet. If we're investing in the right sector, even if the team is more mediocre, or the execution isn't as good, the rising market lifted all the companies in the sector. Some did better than the others, but overall everyone made money.

"We are very thesis driven here. We see a ton of deals from our network, through referrals, or that come in over the transom. However, once a quarter we do a strategic off-site where we'll say, 'Let's pick out some interesting subsectors.' We come up with a thesis that says these are specific pain points; this is how we address them. We outline what we think is the right answer and look for a company in that market. More than half our deals, three or four a year, come out of this process.

"Let's say we were hearing more frequently about managing applications at a data center—that this is a really big problem. We'd have a couple of partners investigate it. They'd call CIOs, go to conferences, and have junior people on our team dig up companies in the market and have them come in. We'd either conclude the market is not interesting or it is interesting, but let's revisit it because it's too early. Or it's interesting, and we've found the right company. Occasionally, we'll conclude it's interesting, but let's go start our own company because we can't find the right investment.

"Our rule of thumb is we'd like the company to get to $100 million in revenue. Realistically, if we can see the company get to $50 million in revenue and the valuation is right, it could still be a good venture deal. In a decent IT market, a $50 million revenue company should be worth at least a $100 million to $200 million outcome. At that point, we're making a good venture multiple, potentially a five to 10 times type of return.

"In today's corporate IT environment, CIOs or VPs of IT have two or three priorities. They're usually willing to pay millions of dollars for those, but beyond that, a $20,000 piece of software might not hit their radar. So, how much a customer is willing to dish out for the solution is a combination of willingness to pay and how high up the pain ladder it is.

"It's a little harder to say what the rule of thumb is on total market size. We've funded some companies that have gone after a $500 million market. But it's a sleepy enough market that we're confident the company can take a big market share. If it's a large entrenched market, we want to see a $1 billion to $2 billion market size so that we can see an opportunity to carve out a slice with a differentiated strategy. There's no easy answer because it gets driven a lot by what the competitive dynamic is. There isn't a table that says if there are 10 competitors, the market size has got to be this much. We're often funding companies in unproven markets, and we just don't know how large the market will be. Frankly, we don't put a lot of weight in market size projections. Usually when someone shows us one, it's 'next slide.' Because everything looks like it's going to be a multibillion-dollar market.

"We don't put much emphasis on legal or patent protection even though we do encourage our companies to try to protect themselves. If a big company comes to steal our company's idea, it might not have the resources to protect itself anyway, so from a market standpoint it may be toast. In the e-commerce days, size and branding were protection from competition. That was unnatural for us and still is unnatural. We think a technology secret sauce is important; it's a bet that people aren't going to solve the problem in a cheap and easy way.

"Again, we go back to the personal aspects of it. Often, the technology isn't there yet, so we're betting that this team can develop it and deliver on it. Coming back to the team issue, we want to make sure they're capable. To the extent there is something to kick the tires on, it's a pretty broad swath. We'll look at the architecture, algorithms, or any kind of secret sauce related to how they approach a particular problem. We'll look at internal processes for development, tools they use, code review, and the philosophy around software development or hardware development because there are different schools out there.

"Here's one that we typically won't do: It looks like a great technology, really groundbreaking, could be a huge market, but it's a technologist—sometimes a wild-eyed technologist—who's driving it. The businessperson is either weak or not there at all. We don't historically play in that situation. We've missed some good things because of it. The hit rate and the time it takes to constantly arm wrestle with the technologist are issues we try to avoid."

How Do You Evaluate the Venture's Prospective Business Model?

"In evaluating a business model, we almost always start on the revenue side to understand the price point and the customer acquisition strategy. As we can see in enterprise software today—and has almost always been the case with systems—a direct sales force is too difficult and expensive to maintain. The days of paying the sales guy a couple hundred thousand bucks a year to go sell a million bucks worth of software are over. Many companies we look at are selling software somewhere between $50,000 to $250,000 a shot. So, it is important to understand whether it is a $20,000 or a $200,000 piece of software.

"How does the company increase the value it gets from a customer? Is it additional modules or more users, and how does that affect pricing? This is really important because that drives the go-to-market strategy—what the sales force and channels look like, and whether the company goes after a small or broad set of customers, and who it sells to in the customer department. These revolve around the pricing strategy. So that's one set of issues.

"The other revolves around the technology side of the business model. What's it going to cost to build this thing—the number of engineers the company needs after it breaks down its various development efforts—and how long will it take to get the product out the door?

"We don't spend too much time initially on the marketing. From a financial standpoint, we look to see if it is a technical sale and how much the ROI [return on investment] calculation comes into play. If it's a hardware business, we need a clear understanding of what working capital looks like. Working capital, especially if the company's doing well, can really be a cash drain.

"We weave this into higher-level issues about how much time we are buying and how much money needs to be raised. We're looking at a company that follows the Salesforce.com model. It is a subscription, hosted software model that looks like it's going to take $7 million to $8 million to get to a decent level of revenue. Right now, it's three guys and a business plan. So the math goes: We'll put in $8 million, probably $10 million to be on the safe side, behind this management team that hasn't really proven much so it's hard to ascribe a value to it. This deal doesn't work financially because we give these guys $3 million to $4 million pre-money value, their ownership would be so small, and they'd have to raise more money down the road and get diluted. That business model is just not fundable. They're trying to recraft it.

"We have always been cautious, and even more so recently, about business models that require a lot of capital to be successful. There are these 'big bang' opportunities where the company is going to build the next server to put Sun out of business. Usually that takes $40 million to $50 million of capital before the investors really know if the company is successful. But the outcome could really be gigantic, right? We typically like the other model of going after a slightly smaller opportunity, a more bite-sized and tactical one. But we'll know early on after $5 million to $7 million of investment if we're on the right track. Then, we hope to get into adjacent markets and grow the company from there."

What Due Diligence Do You Conduct?

"From a due-diligence standpoint, we always have at least two general partners who are sponsors of the company. We also try to have a devil's advocate who is somewhat skeptical to raise objective questions and ensure we've gone through the process. A good example is a company we funded called Clarus up in San Francisco. It's a company that had been around a couple of years before we funded it, and Keith Giarman became CEO. Keith is a classmate from HBS. Clarus is building a software solution to help companies put VoIP [voice-over-Internet protocol] into their businesses. Today, you buy one of Cisco's VoIP phones because they promise savings, but there are problems around voice quality and performance if you change out your switch for your data network.

"We met the founder a couple of times when he was trying to raise his first round of capital. He got some angel funding but wasn't able to raise a venture round. He had a very scrappy team that hadn't made a salary in virtually two years, and the technology was good. The team had moved the product along with some first customers, but the company wasn't fundable in its current state. This is a situation where the founder thought he was going to be the CEO. Two years earlier when we talked, he said he was going to be the CEO. It was apparent after not being able to raise money that he wasn't going to be the CEO.

"The founder came to me six months ago—before we introduced him to Keith—and said he was looking for a CEO, which opened the door. We had an open discussion around Keith as a potential CEO and someone who could help him raise money. Keith had just left a start-up in a related space. I asked him to look at Clarus to see if he was interested. Keith spent four or five weeks at the company digging in and looking at it. He got his arms around it and revamped the story. At that point, we got excited about it and kicked off the formal due-diligence process.

"The product wasn't thrown together, but it wasn't a full enterprise-class-ready product because they didn't have the resources. Specifically, we did a technology drill-down with the team to look at the architecture and the processes. I introduced the Clarus team to the person who runs the telecom network at JP Morgan Chase; he's implementing VoIP there. I also asked him to take a look at the product and give me feedback about big holes, etc.

"Keith had to clean up the management team. We did all our reference calls on the management team, background checks, and criminal tests. That is one thing we never want to get burned on. Funding a felon is a bad bet. Even though we knew Keith, we did make a few more calls. From a legal standpoint, Clarus had signed up a small law firm in the city that did them all kinds of disservice around setting up some poor agreements. So, we had to clean that up as well.

"We also spent a lot of time on the financial model. The key question was how much money should they raise, especially given a new CEO who didn't own the financial plan. Also, it was a situation where it had been a very scrappy team that hadn't been taking full salaries. So all kinds of things could have emerged—oh, this person loaned the company $100,000, or we didn't pay these bills. We find liabilities crop up in situations where the company has been living hand-to-mouth. We spend a lot of time flushing that out.

"From a market standpoint, there were some customer things, but it was more of a bet that this problem was going to continue to emerge. We didn't spend a ton of time talking to Cisco to get its view; we had a pretty good handle on that. I had one of our analysts look for other start-ups. We identified two: one that was a component technology and the second a competitor that some other VCs had funded. There were some bigger guys that had product offerings, but customers and resellers didn't seem to think their products were there yet. We went through the whole process and funded the company with Keith.

"We're trying to find more deals like this where we create the situation ourselves. We know the CEO; we don't have to reference that person. We have also spent time with the technology and the product, and so we put them all together. We have ball control of the deal rather than it being a jump ball with 10 other VCs going after it. The last deal we closed, a video deal, was the same thing.

"In situations where we're betting on momentum, we'll spend a lot of time with the sales team. We'll do account reviews. We'll ask them about the status of their top 20 accounts: where are you, what have you talked about, who are the other guys? We go through the pipeline like we are the VP of sales."

What Is the Process through Which Funding Decisions Are Made?

"I would position Trinity as a moderately sized firm that is fairly traditional in how it approaches the business. We're investing Trinity VIII, a $300 million fund. We call ourselves multistage, but it's all within the realm of early stage. We will do seed investing. Our sweet spot tends to be Series A, the first venture round. But we'll also do follow-on rounds if we think there is a venture multiple involved.

"We try not to do tranched investments, although we have. The danger with tranches is it's very hard not to do that next tranche of capital. There are always reasons something didn't work. We find ourselves in board meetings saying you're right, you're right, okay; let's throw in the next tranche. If we don't fund the tranche then there could be legal repercussions, so we try to avoid it.

"We do try to make each round of financing have enough cushion for the company to hit a major milestone or set of milestones. We don't overfund the first round, and we don't underfund because in this environment it takes between three to six months to fund-raise. We rarely fund a company for less than a year because they're out fund-raising again in six months, perhaps without much to show for it. We're usually looking for an 18-month window."

What Financial Analyses Do You Perform?

"The financial model discussion is more often a good insight into how smart a team is. We don't worry as much about whether their first quarter of revenue is $2 million or $4 million; it's the thinking behind it. When a company says this other company spent X% on sales and marketing so we're going to project that, we don't get a lot of confidence that they know what they're doing. The flip side is when management can give it to us at the line-item level. The team can say, 'When we did our last start-up, we spent $20,000 on this trade show that was worthwhile. We hired these three salespeople, and we paid them this much.' They've got this bottom-up model with every piece falling into place, so we have a lot of confidence they know what they're doing.

"We also try to build a bottom-up projection using empirical data about an analogous problem and solution and what the customer was willing to pay. We estimate how many customers there are to determine how big an opportunity it might be. Since we invest in a relatively focused area of IT,

13

we know that if it's a $200,000 or $300,000 enterprise software solution and a broad enough problem, it's a big enough market. If it's a vertical, then we've got to believe the company's selling a $1 million-plus type solution. So, there are some rules of thumb we adhere to."

What Role Does Risk Play in Your Evaluation?

"There's got to be a clear strategy of managing risk. When we fund a plan, we try to get an internal agreement around the positive thesis and key risks. We outline the action plan to review risk as we go through it. Actually, we also try to make sure the management team is on board because they will execute against it. And that is very explicit. After we've funded, we track our milestones around product, first beta customer, first revenue customer.

"There is a concept of a particular financial return, but it differs from stage to stage. If we look at the three Series As we did last year, the valuations were all in the same ballpark. I don't think we thought this one is a little more risky, this one is a little less risky, and therefore the valuations should reflect it. Within a certain stage of an investment, I think the valuations get driven much more by competitive dynamics than anything else. Ideally, we could be more systematic about the analysis, but in reality, it doesn't play out.

"Last year we did two investments that were second rounds of financing. In both cases, they were companies that were in revenue and starting to ramp. We're willing to pay a higher value for that. They should be lower risk: the dogs were starting to eat the dog food. It was a question of how quickly they'd eat and how well the company would scale from an execution standpoint. In those cases, if we made five times our money we'd probably be happy, but we'd also expect the success rate to be much higher."

How Do You Think about a Potential Exit Route?

"The bulk of companies get acquired, so I think we're pretty realistic about that. On several occasions, we've funded companies we knew were going to be acquired. The odds of going public were pretty slim, but at least they had large, addressable markets so they could get big enough. We need to believe the company is sustainable on its own, rather than timing it so someone acquires it before the company needs more cash.

"An IPO is always the best outcome. It means the company's going to be much bigger. But some of these acquisitions are pretty darn large. We look at what valuation we invest in, and a big part of the equation is how much capital the company needs. I've got a company where the investors invested $110 million, and thus with a $150 million outcome, that's not much of a return. Then we've got other companies where we put in $3 million and own half the company, and if it gets bought at $150 million—that's a huge outcome.

"Part of the reason we have a more moderately sized fund is that our outcomes can have an impact on the fund size. If we had a $1 billion fund, finding an outcome that could have an impact would be really hard; it is still hard with a $300 million fund."

Robert Simon: Director, Alta Partners

Robert Simon joined Alta Partners as a director in 2000 from Sierra Ventures, where he was a venture partner. Simon has 17 years of experience in the software development and Internet sectors

---

14

including starting three companies: DotBank.com, Navitel Communications, and Virgil Corporation. Simon's focus is on information technology, primarily enterprise software. He received a B.S. and M.S. in industrial engineering from Stanford University in 1982 and 1983, respectively.

How Do You Evaluate Potential Venture Opportunities?

"There are two schools of thought. In the first, the venture capitalist says, 'I invest in people first and foremost. Smart people will find great opportunities, and I will never know the sectors or technologies as well as smart people. I back people.' In the other, the venture capitalist says, 'I don't care about people; I care about markets. I look for big opportunities, big painful problems that customers have. If management doesn't work out, I can always fix management.' The truth is obviously somewhere in between, but I'm leaning more on the market side. I think markets trump people and trump technology. We can build something. If no one wants it, we've got a big problem. I've seen that on the entrepreneur side, and now I've seen it on the venture side.

"Under the heading of market, we have customer pain. How much pain does the customer feel, and how much will the customer pay to solve it? We get to market size by estimating how many customers feel the pain. We met with a company here in San Francisco that was developing software for analyzing large log files. Pretty tough stuff, pretty complicated. We asked them about their potential customers. Their solution was best suited to companies that generate a gigabyte a day in log files. How many are there out there? There are two: Yahoo! and eBay. That's a problem.

"On the market side, there are two ways to look at it. The replacement for an existing product is one market: the better, cheaper, faster model. The other is the brave-new-world model where we're introducing a new piece of functionality and don't really know where the markets are. Those tend to fall more on the consumer side. Everybody has an opinion on them because we can relate to them; that's both good and bad. The brave-new-world model certainly has a greater market risk but not necessarily more technical risk. Historically, the venture community has avoided consumer-facing deals for several reasons. The gross margins have typically been pretty slim, the marketing costs are high, and it's a 'hit-driven' business, and we're not good at predicting consumer behavior. Now, on the plus side, we can find consumer-facing deals that are capital efficient. Those are the Internet deals, and some of them have worked out well.

"Everyone wants the $1 billion market. If we're honest, we don't know what and where the $1 billion markets are until we get there. We have to see our way to a $200 million market with the right attributes and a lot of growth potential. We don't target market share for our companies; we target revenue. We expect north of $60 million to $80 million in revenue in three to five years.

"We also look at the technology to see how proprietary and difficult the solution to the problem is. We gauge if we can build defensible barriers. If it's an easy problem that everyone can solve, it's less attractive. The ideal case is four Ph.D.s trying to solve a problem they've been working on for a year or two, and somehow they've struck upon the magic solution. And, it's two orders of magnitude better than whatever else is out there.

"We invested in a company called Aegis that makes an optical component, a tunable filter. The current cost of competitive components is between $2,000 and $5,000. Aegis has developed an almost plug-compatible replacement using a silicon process that puts their cost between $50 and $100. It's a perfect example. The only problem there is the telecom market has fallen off the cliff, so now they have to find new markets.

"Then we look at the people. We want to keep the existing team if possible. They're the ones with the passion and some understanding of the problem. We get a little concerned when the entrepreneur comes in and says, 'I'm in this to flip it in a year.' It rarely works out that way. So if we get the impression they're not in it for the tough times, then it's definitely a problem.

"We have this conversation right up front on their personal motivations, their definition of success, and whether they're wedded to a particular role in the company. We like to avoid a situation where the guy says, 'It's very important for me to be the CEO. It's going to be a big company, and you're either with me or not. You're going to pull me kicking and screaming out of the chair.' So, we say, 'Okay, maybe not a good fit.' Sixty percent of the time or more we're facing a change in management. We want it to be a positive as opposed to a divisive situation for the company.

"Getting back to market versus people and technology, we can have a market where the only issue is the timing. We have an investment in a semiconductor company that's doing a 40-gig network processor. Networking starts out at one megabit, goes to two megabit, 10 megabit, 100 megabit. So all laptops, servers, and switches have 100 megabit connections. The next progression is one gigabit, two gigabit, and we can see our way to 40. Great; we fund it. The only issue is timing: If we're too early, there's no market demand, and we have to survive until the demand reaches us. In that period of time, we have two problems: we have to keep the doors open and feed everybody, and we may be susceptible to being leapfrogged by technology. So we don't want to be too early, but we don't want to be too late."

How Do You Evaluate the Venture's Prospective Business Model?

"I think more of the deals now have clearer business models than the ones from the 1999, 2000, and 2001 period. I think of Hotmail. I know the investors there; they were investors in my previous company. Hotmail never made money; it was acquired for its subscribers rather than its business potential. Microsoft acquired it for $350 million or $450 million; it was one of the first big acquisitions. If you look at that from a classic valuation standpoint, you wouldn't have made the investment. In fact, I had the opportunity and didn't make the investment. Nonetheless, it was a great outcome for the investors. I don't think we want to play that game today because acquisitions are being made for fundamental business reasons rather than other asset reasons. Companies in the Internet space don't feel the need to make those customer acquisition purchases anymore.

"There's a company called Skype that just raised $20 million from Draper Fisher, Tim Draper specifically. I can say this because he's an old college mate. Skype provides the ability to do phone calls over the Net. If both parties have an Internet connection and Skype, they can talk anywhere in the world for the cost of the Internet connection. It's potentially disruptive for international calling, so it potentially has a big market. How Skype makes money is not clear because they don't make money on the calls. Tim Draper is bolder than we are. He's betting that 10 million, at least north of 5 million, people can't be wrong because they're using it, and the company will find a way to monetize that."

What Due Diligence Do You Conduct?

"If I look at a company and like it, I'll do some preliminary due diligence. I'll speak with the entrepreneur by telephone or have them come in. We'll research the company by talking to customers or potential customers to corroborate the customer pain or product utility. We'll ask whether they have experience with the product or service, have they deployed it, and how they would feel if we took it away. If they say they wouldn't care or no way, we can't take it away, that would give us an indication.

"We don't require the company to have paying customers. They can have a pilot or a couple of betas, but we want them to have engaged the customer. We also might introduce them to a portfolio company with the same requirement or CIOs in our network or other potential customers. They'll serve as an off-sheet reference, and we see two things: does the customer confirm and/or have the pain, and how effective is the team at delivering its message.

"We'll also talk to folks who have worked with this particular team and do reference checks on the people. If I really like the company, I'll get another partner engaged. Then, I'll talk up the deal a little bit here and bring it in to the IT partners, which are a smaller set. Finally, as we get more serious, the company will give a presentation to the full partnership in one of our regular Monday meetings. If there are any open issues from that, I'll run them down and bring it back for a decision."

What Is the Process through Which Funding Decisions Are Made?

"Brave-new-world companies are a smaller percentage of our portfolio, although not necessarily a smaller percentage of the deals we see. It's probably worthwhile to put one or two brave-new-world opportunities in a portfolio to see how they end up. The bet can be on the marketing or the technology side. In the brave-new-world case, we start out with a seed investment to see if the company gets any traction. If they can get it deployed, we layer in additional investment once we get some idea about adoption. So we'll seed them with $500,000 or so to get them through product launch, then they'll have to raise money again. Next time, we might go in with $2 million to $4 million.

"There is no set parameter on the amount of capital we invest. Some of it varies by industry. We have to remind ourselves we don't need to invest a ton of money for a software company. I think someone told me PeopleSoft took only $12 million of investment. Adobe only needed $1 million. Adobe got a $1 million advance royalty payment from Apple, but all the equity it needed was $1 million. So I think it's pretty reasonable to do a software company for $15 million to $20 million or less. Telecom systems take more. We may be learning again that they may not be good investments for venture folks because we need 100 to 200 people for 18 to 24 months. That adds up to $200 million and not a happy story—we had one of those.

"We go through a bit of the math with entrepreneurs to show what opportunities are good venture opportunities and what ones are not necessarily good venture opportunities but may still be very good businesses. We can have entrepreneurs who have a $10 million a year business where they own 90%. If it's growing 40% a year, they don't need much capital. So why would they give up half or more of their company to an outside investor? They would have to work at least twice as hard to realize the same personal outcome. Once they take outside investment, they get on this treadmill. Unless they're making progress up that hill, it just becomes a grumpy situation for everybody.

"Across the board, investors are taking anywhere between a month to even six months to make decisions. I had lunch with a guy today who finally did the deal after looking at it for a year. It is more common now to have some time to see the progress a team makes on its own. We meet with the company, and time will pass as we do our research on the opportunity, technology, and customers. Then, we can compare what they actually did with the milestones they set, like signing up a new customer or meeting their quarterly revenue targets."

What Financial Analyses Do You Perform?

"The business presentations usually have both the revenue model and expense model. We first look at the expense model. How much money does the opportunity take to get to cash flow break-even? We construct our own model on revenues because usually they're wildly optimistic: first year $1 million, second year $20 million, third year $100 million—it's a little unrealistic. Often they've also taken a top-down approach on market share. Well, that's all fine and dandy and gives us some idea of market size, but that's really not going to be the revenue ramp. We do a bottom-up analysis for the revenue ramp, and we end up with a fraction of what the top-down is."

What Role Does Risk Play in Your Evaluation?

"Before a decision is made to fund a company, we do a two- to five-page investment memo. There is a section on what we believe the risks are: technical risks, competitive risks, market risks. The financials are not that detailed. They might include revenue over the next four or five years, expenses, etc."

How Do You Think about a Potential Exit Route?

"We'll look at a market size north of $200 million and a company revenue rate north of $60 million to $80 million. We think that will yield a large enough market for an exit. If we can't see the company growing to that size in revenue, then it's probably not an appealing venture investment. And before we go into an investment, we'll definitely have a conversation about who would be likely acquirers, who would be good partners.

"Timing an exit is a bit of a dicey thing. Building lasting companies that continue to grow consistently over time is a more reliable way to make money than getting out just in time."

Exhibit 1   Venture Capital Firm Background Information

Kleiner Perkins Caufield & Byers (KPCB)—Founded in 1972, KPCB has helped entrepreneurs build over 400 companies including America Online, Sun Microsystems, Amazon, Juniper, and Genentech. It closed its $400 million Kleiner Perkins Caufield & Byers XI fund in February 2004. The partners expect to fund emerging growth companies in information technology, life sciences, and other fast-growing industries over a three-year period. KPCB's current portfolio includes companies in the following sectors: broadband equipment and services, consumer devices and services, enterprise software and services, financial services, Internet infrastructure software and services, medical devices, heath-care services, and biotech. In its office on Sand Hill Road in Menlo Park, KPCB has six partners emeritus and 17 investment professionals: 12 partners, one principal, and four associate partners.

Menlo Ventures—Menlo Ventures has seven funds with $2.7 billion under management invested in over 270 companies. Founded in 1976, Menlo Ventures invests in communications, Internet infrastructure, software, semiconductor, data storage, and computer hardware companies. Menlo Ventures typically invests $5 million to $10 million at the start-up phase of a company and $10 million to $25 million at later stages. It is willing to invest in all stages of a U.S.-headquartered private company's growth. Portfolio successes include LSI Logic, UUNET Technologies, Hotmail Corporation, and Clarify. Located on Sand Hill Road in Menlo Park, California, Menlo Ventures has 14 investment professionals: seven managing directors, four associates, and three investment analysts.

Trinity Ventures—Founded in 1986, Trinity Ventures primarily invests in early-stage and emerging growth technology companies. Trinity Fund VIII has approximately $300 million of committed capital to fund opportunities in the following sectors: software, services, communications and networked systems, and semiconductors. Portfolio company successes include Blue Nile (IPO), Crescendo (acquired by Cisco), Network Alchemy (acquired by Nokia), P.F. Chang's (IPO), Starbucks (IPO), and Wall Data (IPO). Located on Sand Hill Road in Menlo Park, California, Trinity's team consists of six general partners, one venture partner, one principal, and one analyst.

Alta Partners—Since its inception in 1996, Alta Partners has funded approximately 120 early- and later-stage life sciences and early-stage information technology companies. Alta manages seven venture funds approximating $1.5 billion in committed capital including $475 million in two life sciences funds that closed in March 2004. Alta's geographic focus is U.S. companies, although it has made selective investments in Europe. Alta's IPOs in 2004 include Corgentech, Eyetech Pharmaceuticals, and Renovis. Prior investments in the information technology sector include Be, Inc. (acquired by Palm Computing), Coloma Wireless (acquired by AT&T), and Fibex Systems (acquired by Cisco Systems). Located in San Francisco, Alta Partners has 10 professionals devoted to life sciences (eight directors and two principals) and four directors in information technology.

Source: Adapted from venture capital firm bios at www.kpcb.com, www.menloventures.com, www.trinityventures.com, www.altapartners.com.

ROBIN GREENWOOD

MICHAEL GORZYNSKI

H Partners and Six Flags

In December 2009, Rehan Jaffer and Usman Nabi had a difficult choice to make. Jaffer, the chief investment officer of H Partners, a New York-based hedge fund, and Nabi, his partner, had been meeting over dinner with Arik Ruchim, an analyst at the firm. H Partners had invested a significant amount of the firm's capital in the senior bonds of U.S.-based Six Flags, following that company's bankruptcy filing. Six Flags was one of the largest amusement park operators in the world, managing 20 parks in the United States, Canada and Mexico, and entertaining over 25 million visitors per year. As Six Flags' revenue fell in early 2009, the company had fallen into distress, finding it difficult to make payments on $2.7 billion of debt and preferred stock. At the same time, global debt markets were experiencing turmoil, making it challenging for the company to refinance. Facing imminent maturity on $308 million of preferred shares, on June 13, 2009, Six Flags filed for Chapter 11 protection under the US bankruptcy code. H Partners had acquired some of Six Flags' senior bonds immediately after the Company's bankruptcy filing at approximately 60% of par value.

H Partners' investment had proven to be a prescient one, as capital markets began to slowly open up to companies like Six Flags in late 2009. By December, as the company progressed through the bankruptcy process, the market reflected greater value in the senior bonds (see **Exhibit 1**).

Jaffer and Nabi were happy with the performance of the Six Flags senior bonds, but wondered whether their investment had run its course. Perhaps there were additional opportunities available within the company's capital structure? The H Partners team was wary, however, because the bonds, as well as the company as a whole, had increased in value considerably. At the same time, Six Flags had not reported a profit in the last seven years. As Jaffer, Nabi, and Ruchim finished dinner in the restaurant in the lobby of their building on 7th Avenue, they discussed whether it was time to focus on H Partners' other investments.

H Partners

Jaffer began his career as an analyst at investment bank Donaldson, Lufkin & Jenrette (DLJ) in Los Angeles. During the late 1990s, he helped companies issue junk bonds to finance their growth.

A couple of years into his job, in 2001 Jaffer met hedge fund investor Daniel Loeb in DLJ's New York offices. Loeb was the founder and Chief Investment Officer of Third Point, a value-oriented hedge fund focused on "special situations", including the securities of distressed companies. Jaffer and Loeb both foresaw a series of bankruptcies among telecommunications companies as the economy declined. Loeb persuaded Jaffer to join Third Point, to help the fund invest in distressed companies.

Professor Robin Greenwood and Visiting Scholar Michael Gorzynski (MBA 2007) prepared this case with the assistance of Research Associate Julie Messina (MBA 2001). HBS cases are developed solely as the basis for class discussion. Cases are not intended to serve as endorsements, sources of primary data, or illustrations of effective or ineffective management.

After joining Third Point in 2001, Jaffer helped select investments in distressed bonds, including those of some of the same companies he had helped to finance earlier in his career. Over the next few years, Jaffer helped the fund make profitable investments in companies such as Dade-Behring, Magellan, Warnaco, and Leap Wireless.

In January 2005, Jaffer left Third Point to found H Partners with an initial investment of $15 million, comprised of his own savings and capital from friends and family. Jaffer's fund would focus on investments in small and mid-sized restructurings. From the beginning, Jaffer planned to re-apply the strategy he had learned from the 2001 to 2004 distressed cycle.

Between 2005 and 2010, H Partners generated compound annual net returns of 24%. During this time, Jaffer grew the fund's assets under management to $800 million, comprised of capital from employees, wealthy families and endowments. In addition, he expanded the team to 10 employees. Jaffer's partner Nabi joined the firm in 2006 from the hedge fund Perry Capital. **Exhibit 2** summarizes the professional backgrounds of members of the H Partners team.

Investment Process

In 2010, H Partners focused its investing efforts on debt in distressed companies, as well as post-bankruptcy and reorganization ("post reorg") equities. In its debt investments, the fund sought to buy debt at significant discounts to par value, and recover value through its understanding of the bankruptcy and reorganization process. In its post-reorg equity investments, the fund aimed to capitalize on low valuations the market placed on the equity of firms as they emerged from bankruptcy. The fund usually maintained a concentrated portfolio, with the top 10 positions comprising 80% of the fund.

Based on his experiences at Third Point, Jaffer believed that the taint of bankruptcy could remain with companies despite structural improvements established in bankruptcy. For example, Jaffer had observed that many post-bankruptcy companies traded at discounts to comparable publicly listed firms. In part, this reflected the riskiness of investing in these companies, as these companies occasionally slid back into distress. But Jaffer had found that the long-horizon returns of these companies significantly exceeded that of peer firms. And, as these companies surprised investors with strong financial performance, the valuation discount tended to dissipate.

Jaffer believed that value could be identified through a careful understanding of the bankruptcy process. In selecting potential investments for the fund, Jaffer, Nabi and the rest of the H Partners team searched for companies meeting the following four criteria:

(1) **Business quality:** The business could not be in secular decline. Jaffer felt it was possible to distinguish between firms which had encountered financial distress as a result of one-time events, cyclical pressures, or excessive leverage, and firms which had entered bankruptcy because of a secular deterioration in the underlying business.

(2) **Liability restructuring:** The restructuring would have to eliminate significant liabilities, making the business stronger going forward. According to Nabi, "bankruptcy allows companies to reduce debt and shed loss making businesses." Adding, "taking advantage of net operating loss carry forwards (NOLs) reduces taxes going forward and allows companies to deliver very quickly."

(3) **Price dislocations:** Investor behavior caused potential price dislocations. Jaffer noted that as a company became distressed, certain lenders who had acquired a company's loans at par, such as collateralized loan obligations (CLOs) might not be able to hold the debt once it had defaulted. Explained Jaffer, "Sometimes you know the seller is smart and sophisticated, but

2

they have to sell." Similarly, as a company emerged from the bankruptcy process, former creditors were often forced to sell the newly emerged equity because of institutional restrictions such as a bank not being allowed to hold equity. Moreover, some interested buyers such as private equity firms faced restrictions in their involvement in the bankruptcy process. H Partners focused on finding the few situations where institutional incentives created a "gap" for H Partners, allowing the fund to step in to buy assets at a discount.

(4) **Management incentives:** Jaffer and Nabi evaluated the background and incentives facing the board of directors and management. Humbled by the experience of bankruptcy, management projections were often conservative. In addition, management teams were often incented to provide conservative forecasts to increase the future value of stock-based compensation received upon emergence from bankruptcy. Jaffer's team always made a point of examining the incentive plans of management teams and the composition of the company's board. This allowed them to understand whether management and the board were sufficiently aligned with the interests of shareholders.

When the 2008 recession began, the H Partners team picked through small and mid-cap restructurings in the U.S. to identify opportunities. The distressed cycle was more severe than anything Jaffer or Nabi had expected, with hundreds of distressed situations to look through (see **Exhibit 3** for a list of major chapter 11 filings, and **Exhibit 4** summarizes the returns of selected post-reorg equities during the 2001-2004 distressed cycle).

Investing in distressed securities was a competitive business, with many hedge funds and private equity firms interested in extracting value from the bankruptcy process. Yet, the landscape of firms H Partners competed against had changed over the years. Many of the funds which had successfully invested in distressed companies during the 2001-2004 distressed cycle had since become much larger, and were thus less interested in "midmarket" transactions. Other funds had a short-term focus. Jaffer and Nabi felt certain they could exploit their edge in these situations.

Six Flags

Six Flags was founded in 1961 with one theme park in Arlington, Texas. Over the next several decades, the company expanded throughout the U.S. and internationally through acquisitions. By 2009, the Company was the largest regional theme park operator in the world, measured by the number of properties, and fourth by number of visitors.[1] The company owned or operated 20 parks in markets across North America, attracting 25.3 million visitors in 2008. The company employed over 2,000 full-time employees, and approximately 27,000 seasonal workers.[2]

Six Flags' parks offered a complete "family-oriented entertainment experience" with a broad selection of thrill rides, water attractions, themed areas, concerts and shows, restaurants, game venues and retail outlets. During 2008, Six Flags theme parks offered more than 800 rides, including over 120 roller coasters, making Six Flags the leading provider of thrill rides in the industry (see **Exhibit 5**).

The Company's parks were located in diverse markets across North America, with no single park accounting for more than 13% of revenue or 18% of Modified EBITDA in 2008.[3] The parks were

---

[1] Park World, "TEA/ERA Attraction Attendance Report 2007,"
http://www.connectingindustry.com/downloads/pwteaerasupp.pdf, accessed March 2011.

[2] Six Flags, 2007 10-K filing, p. 15.

[3] Modified EBITDA = EBITDA before minority interest adjustments.

primarily marketed to guests who live within 100 miles, and the Company's primary markets included nine of the top ten designated market areas in the United States.[4] **Exhibit 6** shows a list of Six Flags major properties.

Amusement and theme parks featured "thrill rides" and attractions set in a park like environment. In 2007, the industry consisted of thousands of small operators, but the top five players accounted for 46% of the market. The primary drivers of revenue in the theme park business were ticket sales and in-park spending which came from visitor spending on food concessions, merchandise, and games. Ticket prices averaged substantially below posted gate prices, because the parks ran significant promotions and group discounts to drive traffic. Average ticket prices in 2008 were $21.10.

Six Flags management felt that theme park attendance was driven by the quality of the park experience.[5] Parks used new rides and attractions to drive attendance rates up. Thus, the parks required regular capital expenditures and access to real estate. The parks also sought to increase spending while customers were in the park, by maximizing the number of hours spent inside.

Management believed high barriers to entry protected each of the Company's parks from new theme park competition. Restricted supply of real estate and zoning restrictions limited the likelihood of new entrants. In addition, high initial capital investment and long "lead-times" prevented competitors from entering the market. Between 1998 and 2009, the total number of major regional theme parks in the US was unchanged.

Between 2003 and 2009, Six Flags' financial performance was volatile, with several owners and management teams attempting a series of financial and operational restructurings. By 2004, Six Flags began closing and selling properties to address the Company's ballooning debt problem. In 2005, several of Six Flags' major investors—fed up with what they viewed as mismanagement—launched a proxy contest to take over the board of the company.[6] Red Zone, LLC, the investment vehicle of entrepreneur Daniel Snyder (which owned 12% of Six Flags at the time), took control of the company's board, with support from shareholders including Cascade Investments. CEO Kieran Burke was replaced with Mark Shapiro, previously a programming executive at television network ESPN.

Shapiro and the company's new board established a new strategy to grow Six Flags into a global entertainment company. In 2007, Six Flags invested $40 million to acquire a stake in Dick Clark Productions, a television production company, and in 2009, the company leveraged the Six Flags brand with the opening of Roller Coaster Cuts, a chain of haircutting salons for children. Shapiro explained the rationale: "Six Flags reaches people in a way that no one else does. And we need to trade on that currency. We need to grow the business, our reach, construct new platforms, stretch the brand in search of new revenue streams. Really in this day and age we have to be a social network."[7] In addition, Shapiro and his team invested significant cash to "clean up" the parks. Jeff Speed, Six Flags' CFO explained the strategy: "We really had to shock the system, so to speak, in 2006 and 2007 with increased operating costs, product enhancements, staffing initiatives and marketing spend given where the brand and the park experience was. As validated by our record guest satisfaction scores, we've been successful in re-establishing a quality park experience and improved brand image."[8]

---

[4] A "designated market area" or "DMA" is a region where the population can receive the same media offerings.

[5] Six Flags, 2007 Annual Report, p. 1.

[6] Six Flags, 2006 10-K filing, p.7.

[7] Six Flags Conference Call, June 21, 2007.

[8] Six Flags Earnings Conference Call, November 9, 2007.

4

Management Initiates Exchange Offer

Six Flags began 2009 with over $2.7 billion of debt and preferred stock. The company faced the maturity of $308 million in preferred stock in August of that year, with another $131 million of bonds maturing in 2010.

Six Flags' pre-bankruptcy capital structure is summarized in **Exhibit 7**. Six Flags Theme Parks ("SFTP") bank debt was secured directly by the Company's assets and held primarily by banks. Six Flags Operations ("SFO") notes were unsecured bonds, held primarily by investment management firms. Finally, Six Flags Inc. ("SFI") notes were the most junior bonds, consisting of convertible and straight unsecured bonds. These were primarily held by investment management firms, as shown in **Exhibit 8**.

In April 2009, Six Flags management attempted to restructure the company's financial obligations via a debt-for-equity exchange offer. An exchange offer was a typical first step in a restructuring process, as management would attempt to restructure a company's balance sheet out of court. In the proposed offer, the bank debt and SFO bonds were to remain in place, while 85% of the equity in the business was assigned to the SFI bonds, 10% to the preferred shares, and 5% to the common equity holders. The implied enterprise value was $1.7 billion.

However, it was Jaffer's experience that exchange offers were rarely successful, because they required a high threshold of acceptance by creditors in all classes (95% in the case of Six Flags). Differing maturities on the various bond issues within the SFI class caused the exchange offer to fail as holders of bonds maturing in 2010 demanded preferential treatment to holders of longer-dated bonds, and ultimately rejected the offer. Jaffer noted, "Certain holders of the SFI notes maturing in 2010 demanded a premium to holders of the 2013, 2014 and 2015 notes." Believing that the exchange offer was likely to fail, Jaffer, Nabi and Ruchim conducted an extensive due diligence process so that H Partners would be prepared to act quickly if Six Flags filed for bankruptcy.

Bankruptcy

Following the failed exchange offer, the Company's operating performance continued to deteriorate in early 2009. Theme park attendance dropped for several reasons, including the onset of the H1N1 "swine flu" virus (which caused the Mexico City park to shut down for two weeks and impacted the two Texas parks), inclement weather, and negative media reports surrounding the company's impending bankruptcy. Attendance between April and June declined by 800,000 visitors year-over-year. In addition, a deteriorating economy led to lower in-park revenues, as average guest spending declined by 3%.

At the same time, global capital markets were in disarray in early 2009, and Six Flags approached several important maturities. By June, Six Flags management decided that an out of court settlement was no longer feasible. As several grace periods for interest payments were about to expire, on June 13, 2009, the company filed for bankruptcy protection.

About Chapter 11

Under Chapter 11 of the U.S. Bankruptcy Code, companies which were unable to pay their debts were permitted to file for protection from creditors. In many cases, management would continue to operate the company while developing a plan to reorganize the company's finances.

Debt restructuring was subject to approval by the Bankruptcy Court, and accomplished through the use of a Bankruptcy Plan. During the first 120 days following the bankruptcy petition, the debtor (e.g. Six Flags existing management and board) had the exclusive right to file a plan of reorganization. The Bankruptcy Court could extend this "exclusivity period" for up to 18 months. The plan was accompanied by a disclosure statement which described the debtor's financial circumstances, including the financial structure of the company pre-filing, the treatment of the creditors, projections of earnings, and a discussion of options. Any plan under consideration would have to be voted upon by the creditors.

During the reorganization process, claims against the company would be classified into classes of differing priority. The bankruptcy plan would specify the treatment given each class. For a plan to be confirmed by the bankruptcy court, it would have to be accepted by at least one class of *impaired* claims, and by a 2/3 majority in dollar amount of such claims. Impaired claims were the claims of creditors that would not, under the plan, be paid in full.

Creditors could object to the confirmation of the debtor's plan. For example, they might challenge the debtor's valuation of their collateral, or the feasibility of the plan. The debtor would typically provide creditors with detailed financial projections to assist the bankruptcy court in determining whether the business could be successfully restructured.

Because the most junior claimants in a bankruptcy expected to have their claims wiped out, they would often vote against plans put together by management or the senior creditors. To solicit their support and prevent hold up of the bankruptcy process, more senior creditors would agree to let the junior claimants share the pool. However, even if a class voted against a plan, the court could still approve the plan if it found a plan to be "fair and equitable," and not unfairly discriminating against any particular class. This was called a "cram down."

Management Plan

When he woke up on the morning of Saturday, June 13th, 2009, Ruchim was not surprised to learn that Six Flags had filed for bankruptcy. However, when he reviewed the terms of the plan of reorganization, he was shocked. The implied enterprise value had declined by 25%, from $1.7 billion to $1.25 billion. Whereas the exchange offer assigned 85% of the equity to the SFI bonds, the reorganization plan assigned only 1% to this class. Bank lenders would receive a new $600 million term loan as well as 92% of the equity; SFO bonds would receive 7% of the equity; SFI bonds would receive 1% of the equity; and preferred and common stock would receive nothing. In addition, the Long-Term Incentive Plan awarded the top seven executives with 3.75% of the equity in restricted stock and another 3.75% in options, which diluted debt holders, and Daniel Snyder would remain as Chairman of the Board (see **Exhibit 9** for Six Flags management and board prior to bankruptcy).

As news of the bankruptcy plan was interpreted by the market, Six Flags' bond and stock prices fell dramatically. H Partners acquired Six Flags' SFO bonds immediately after the bankruptcy filing, at approximately 60% of par value.

H Partners Invests in Six Flags

Nabi and Ruchim studied the financial performance of Six Flags prior to bankruptcy, comparing it to peers and taking into account the depressed state of the economy. They wondered whether the business was in secular decline, or simply overextended. They noted that over the past ten years, the business had an average enterprise value of $3.3 billion, and that the theme park business had been resilient during recessionary periods. Since 1990, U.S. theme park spending had increased every year, with an average growth rate of 4.5%. Attendance had increased in 17 of the past 19 years, with an average growth rate of 1.8%.[9] Dips in attendance tended to rebound as the economy recovered, or as one-time weather events did not repeat. For example, attendance declined 2.9% in 1994 but rebounded by 4.9% in 1995. Attendance again declined 0.6% in 2003 but rebounded 1.9% in 2004. Six Flags' attendance was down nearly 6% in 2009.

Nabi and Ruchim assessed Six Flags' competitive position in the theme park industry. The barriers to entry were significant. Even if a competitor had the necessary land and permits, Six Flags management estimated that it would take at least two years and cost more than $300 million to construct a single theme park.[10] To build Six Flags' major parks could require as much as $5 billion. Nabi and Ruchim had visited all of Six Flags' major parks during the diligence process. Ruchim noted that the parks "are in great condition and loaded with the newest rides." Adding, "the parks are well manicured and very clean, in stark contrast to what I recall from visiting the parks as a kid."

Finally, Nabi and Ruchim analyzed Six Flags' non-core assets, which included a $1.3 billion NOL and over 1,000 acres of excess land. They believed that the NOL would survive the bankruptcy and, as a result, the company would pay minimal taxes for the foreseeable future.[11]

Six Flags' operating performance, however, was a concern. After a weak start to the 2009 season, Six Flags' performance had remained depressed. In November 2009, management expected 2009 revenues to be down 10.4% ($105.7 million) from the prior year, with ticket sales down 8.5% ($45.6 million), and in-park spending down 10.2% ($43.5 million). Cedar Fair, a comparable regional theme park operator of 11 amusement parks and 7 water parks, was experiencing similar revenue declines to Six Flags, but expected 2009 EBITDA to decline only 13% versus Six Flags' 31% projected decline. Cedar Fair had reduced cash operating expenses by $28.6 million, or 5%, during the first nine months of 2009. In contrast, Six Flags management forecast the company's cash operating expenses to decline by $2.4 million in 2009, or 0.4%. **Exhibit 11** summarizes historical financial data for both Six Flags and Cedar Fair.

Long-term expectations had also changed. In an April 2008 presentation, Six Flags' CEO presented a scenario in which the business would generate $440 million in 2011 EBITDA.[12] The Company's November 2009 projections forecast $281 million in 2011 EBITDA, 36% less than the previous estimate (see **Exhibit 12**).[13]

SFO Plan

Meanwhile, global equity markets had partially recovered, with the S&P 500 index up by over 20 percent since Six Flags' initial bankruptcy filing. Debt markets had begun to reopen for competitors to Six Flags. Theme parks had historically supported high leverage due to their ownership of land and structures, which could be liquidated to pay bondholders. On October 7th, Blackstone purchased Sea World and Busch Gardens with leverage of 4.1 times EBITDA.[14] Two weeks later, Universal Orlando issued high yield debt with leverage of 5.9 times EBITDA, and in mid-December 2009, the

---

[9] PricewaterhouseCoopers' 2007-2011 Global Entertainment and Media Outlook Report, p. 610.

[10] Six Flags, 2009 10-K report, p.2.

[11] Disclosure Statement for Debtors' Second Amended Joint Plan of Reorganization, Case No. 09-12019, pp. 119-120.

[12] Six Flags Management Presentation, from 4/29/08 8-K filing, http://www.sec.gov/Archives/edgar/data/70134/000091412108000377/p12706720-ex99_1.pdf.

[13] Six Flags, 2010 8-K filing, p.47.

[14] William Spain, "Blackstone to buy A-B InBev's theme parks for $2.7 billion," MarketWatch, October 7, 2009.

7

private equity fund Apollo Management L.P. offered to acquire Cedar Fair with leverage of 5.5 times EBITDA.[15]

Exploiting improved credit markets, SFO bond holders, of which H Partners was the third largest, convinced management that they had a fully-funded plan which provided higher recoveries to creditors. On November 7, 2009, Six Flags filed a new plan of reorganization with the Bankruptcy Court. As part of the reorganization, SFO bond holders made arrangements for J.P. Morgan, Bank of America, Barclays and Deutsche Bank to provide $830 million in a secured credit facility to finance the company's exit from bankruptcy. The facilities consisted of a $150 million in a revolving credit facility, as well as a $680 million term loan. In addition, SFO bond holders would contribute up to $450 million of new equity through a rights offering.[16]

Confirmation of the plan of reorganization was expected to occur in March 2010, with Six Flags emerging from bankruptcy shortly thereafter. The plan assigned 95% of the Company's equity to SFO bondholders and 5% to SFI bondholders. As banks were to be repaid in full, they were deemed to be "unimpaired" and therefore not entitled to vote on the plan. Plan enterprise value had increased from $1.25 billion to approximately $1.4 billion.

The Long-Term Incentive Plan would remain in place and dilute debt holders. Daniel Snyder would be replaced as Chairman of the Board by Marc Lasry, founder of hedge fund Avenue Capital.

Decision

While H Partners had enjoyed some success with their investment in the SFO bonds, Jaffer's team needed to decide what to do next.

One option was to close their position in the bonds, realizing a substantial gain. This option looked attractive for a number of reasons. Six Flags' historical performance was poor and several management teams had attempted to improve profitability with little success. Moreover, the macroeconomic environment remained uncertain: a reversal in the capital markets would significantly impede Six Flags' ability to refinance its balance sheet.

A second option was to participate in the SFO rights offering, thereby maintaining the third largest ownership position in the post-reorganization equity. But this would entail taking on more exposure to Six Flags, and thus more risk.

A third option was to move down the capital structure to buy more junior securities. These securities, which traded at 20% of face value, had the potential of becoming equity in the reorganization.

A last option was to do nothing now, and wait until Six Flags emerged from bankruptcy. This might afford H Partners the chance to buy equity soon after listing. Jaffer and Nabi had studied many bankruptcy situations, and suspected that some of the same price dynamics which had occurred during bankruptcy might happen again. Jaffer thought that these dynamics might allow H Partners to buy equity in the new firm at a significant discount.

---

[15] Cedar Fair Form 8-K (current report) filed with Securities and Exchange Commission, December 17, 2009.

[16] Disclosure Statement for Debtors' Second Amended Joint Plan of Reorganization, Case No. 09-12019, pp. 119-120.

8

Exhibit 1a   Six Flags Bond Prices (SFO denotes the senior debt)

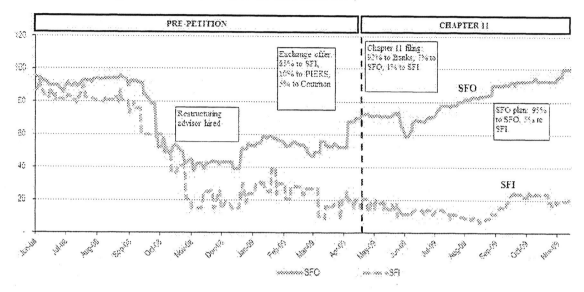

Source: Bloomberg and Casewriters' Analysis.

Exhibit 1b   Six Flags Equity prices

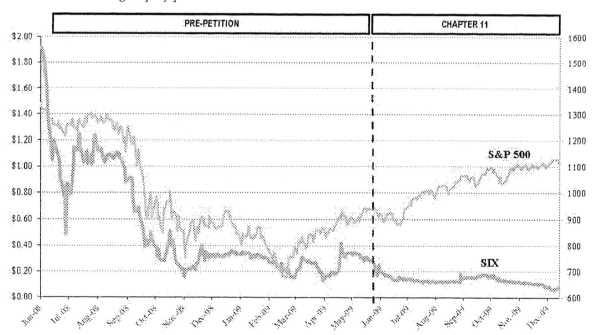

Source: Center for Research on Securities Prices and Casewriters' Analysis.

Exhibit 2   H Partners Team

Rehan Jaffer   Third Point
                         Donaldson, Lufkin & Jenrette (DLJ)

Usman Nabi   Perry Capital
                         Carlyle Group
                         Lazard Freres

Arik Ruchim   Viacom
                         Creative Artists Agency

Lloyd Blumberg   Third Point
                         Arthur Anderson

Meghan Brodbeck   Citco Fund Services

Heather Broome   River Run
                         Citibank

Derrick Chu   Bain Capital
                         Bain & Company

Whitney Cook   Microstrategy

Darren Dinneen   Makena Capital
                         Aetos Capital

Matthew Spiegelman   Morgan Stanley
                         Conference Board

Source: Company documents.

Exhibit 3   Major Corporate Chapter 11 filings, 2008-2009

TOUSA, (OTC:TOUS.Q)	ER Urgent Care Holdings(OTC:RUC)	Tumbleweed (OTC:TMBL.Q)
Manchester, (OTC:MNCS.Q)	Paladin Holdings (OTC:PLHI)	Charter Communications
Sharper Image (OTC:SHRP.Q)	Chapeau (OTC:CPEU)	Vermillion, (NasdaqGM:VRML)
Electro-Chemical Tech.	Reinsurance Technologies	Sun-Times Media Group
Osyka (OTC:OSKA)	MPC (OTC:MPCC.Q)	SuperMedia (NasdaqGS:SPMD)
Thinkpath (OTC:THPH.F)	Harold's Stores (OTC:HRLS.Q)	Wow Entertainment
CenterStaging (OTC:CNSC)	Xechem International	Aventine Renewable Energy
Galaxy Energy (OTC:GAXI.Q)	MicroIslet, (OTC:MIIS)	AbitibiBowater, (NYSE:ABH)
Cygnus eTransaction Group	Circuit City Stores (OTC:CCTY.Q)	Thornburg Mortgage (OTC:THMR.Q)
Lexington Precision (OTC:LEXP.Q)	Accentia Biopharm. (OTC:ABPI)	Energy Partners (NYSE:EPL)
The Fashion House Holdings,	Redroller Holdings (OTC:RROL.Q)	Adfitech, (OTC:ADFT)
RedEnvelope (OTC:REDE.Q)	Vubotics, (OTC:VBTC)	RR Valve,
Verso Technologies (OTC:VRSO.Q)	Hawaiian Telcom (OTC:HWLT)	BankUnited Financial
Tarpon Industries	Pilgrim's Pride (NYSE:PPC)	Visteon (NYSE:VC)
Steakhouse Partners (OTC:STKP.Q)	Platina Energy Grp, (OTC:PLTG.Q)	Dex One (NYSE:DEXO)
Digital Gas	Introgen Therapeutics	Particle Drilling Tech (OTC:PDRT)
Security Intelligence Technologies	Molecular Imaging (OTC:MLRI.Q)	Motors Liq. Co. (OTC:MTLQ.Q)
Torrent Energy (OTC:TREN.Q)	PFF Bancorp (OTC:PFFB.Q)	Six Flags Entertainment (NYSE:SIX)
Distributed Energy Systems	Telemetrix (OTC:TLXT.Q)	SendTec (OTC:SNDN)
Tekoil & Gas (OTC:TKGN)	DnC Multimedia (OTC:DCNM.Q)	Fibrocell Science, (OTC:FCSC)
EarthFirst Technologies (OTC:EFTI)	Scantek Medical (OTC:SKML.Q)	FIRSTPLUS Financial Group
Signature Group Holdings Inc	The Parent Co. (OTC:KIDS.Q)	QSGI, (OTC:QSGI.Q)
Whitehall Jewelers Hlds,	Chesapeake (OTC:CSKE.Q)	Montgomery Realty Group
Shoe Pavilion (OTC:SHOE.Q)	Constar International (OTC:CNST.Q)	Lear (NYSE:LEA)
Fearless International, (OTC:FRLE)	Tronox (OTC:TROX)	Sound Health Sols, (OTC:SHSO)
BAXL Holdings, (OTC:BXLH)	Golden Minerals Co. (AMEX:AUMN)	Luna Innovations Inc
Bonnette & Picard, LLC	Hartmarx (OTC:HTMX.Q)	EC Development, (OTC:ECDI)
Ascendia Brands, (OTC:ASCB.Q)	Smurfit-Stone Container	Web Press (OTC:WEBP.Q)
Atlantis Plastics (OTC:ATPL)	Global Aircraft Sols., (OTC:GACF.Q)	GPS Industries (OTC:GPSN.Q)
Affinity Technology Group	IdentiPHI, (OTC:IDPI.Q)	Cooper-Standard Holdings
Lehman Brothers Holdings	Young Broadcasting (OTC:YBTV.Q)	Astrata Group (OTC:ATTG.Q)
CrossPoint Energy Co.	Rexhall Industries (OTC:REXL.Q)	Colonial Bancgroup
American Ammunition	Bullion River Gold (OTC:BLRV.Q)	Guaranty Financial Group
Washington Mutual (OTC:WAMU.Q)	Spansion (NYSE:CODE)	Southern Community Newspapers
Tatonka Oil & Gas, (OTC:TTKA)	SLS International (OTC:SLSZ.Q)	Barzel Industries (OTC:TPUT.Q)
SurgiLight (OTC:SLGT.Q)	Sterling Mining Co. (OTC:SRLM.Q)	CIB Marine Bancshares (OTC:CIBH)
TVIA	Primus Telecommunications Group	Velocity Express (OTC:VEXP.Q)
WorldSpace, (OTC:WRSP.Q)	Chemtura (NYSE:CHMT)	Stamford Ind. Grp, (OTC:SIDG.Q)
TWL (OTC:TWLO)	Tapestry Pharmaceuticals	Accuride (NYSE:ACW)
Modtech Holdings, (OTC:MODT.Q)	Meruelo Maddux Properties	Sterling Energy Rsrcs (SGER.Q)
		Fairpoint Comm, (NasdaqCM:FRP)

Source: Capital IQ, accessed March 2011.

Exhibit 4a   Post-reorg Equities Returns (2001-2004 Distressed Cycle)

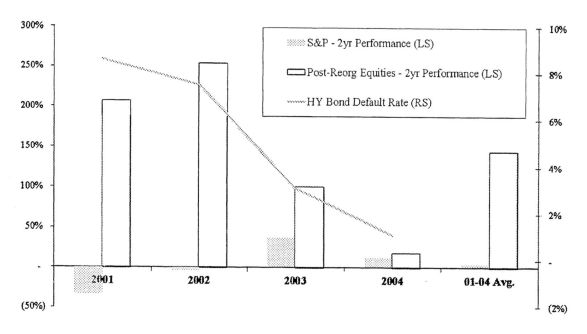

Source: Bloomberg and Casewriter Analysis.

Exhibit 4b   Distribution of Post-reorg Equities Returns (2001-2004 Distressed Cycle)

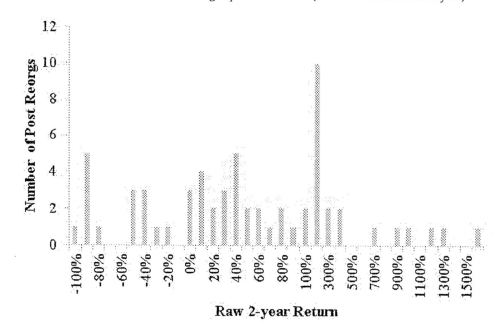

Source: Bloomberg and Casewriter Analysis.

12

Exhibit 5   Six Flags Theme Park Attractions

Source: Six Flags, 2010 8-K filing.

Exhibit 6   Six Flags Properties

Park	Location	2008 Revenue ($M)	Acreage	Population within: 50 Miles	100 Miles	Estimated Replacement Cost ($M)
Six Flags America	Largo, Maryland	45	523	7.0	11.7	100
Six Flags Discovery Kingdom	Vallejo, California	60	138	5.5	10.2	250
Six Flags Fiesta Texas	San Antonio, Texas	75	224	2.1	3.7	400
Six Flags Great Adventure/HH/Wild Safari	Jackson, New Jersey	140	2,200	13.7	27.2	600
Six Flags Great America	Gurnee, Illinois	120	304	8.5	13.1	500
The Great Escape & Splashwater Kingdom	Lake George, New York	45	351	1.1	3.1	250
Six Flags Magic Mountain/HH	Valencia, California	125	262	10.6	17.8	600
Six Flags Mexico	Mexico City, Mexico	60	110	30.0	42.0	350
Six Flags Over Georgia/Whitewater	Austell, Georgia	80	359	4.2	7.0	500
Six Flags Over Texas/HH	Arlington, Texas	95	264	6.5	7.1	530
Six Flags St. Louis	Eureka, Missouri	40	497	2.6	3.8	400
Six Flags New England	Agawam, Massachusetts	70	284	3.1	15.2	200
La Ronde	Montreal, Canada	50	146	4.3	5.8	200
			5,662	99.2	167.7	4,880

Source: Six Flags, 2010 8-K filing and H Partners Estimates.

Exhibit 7 Six Flags Capital Structure

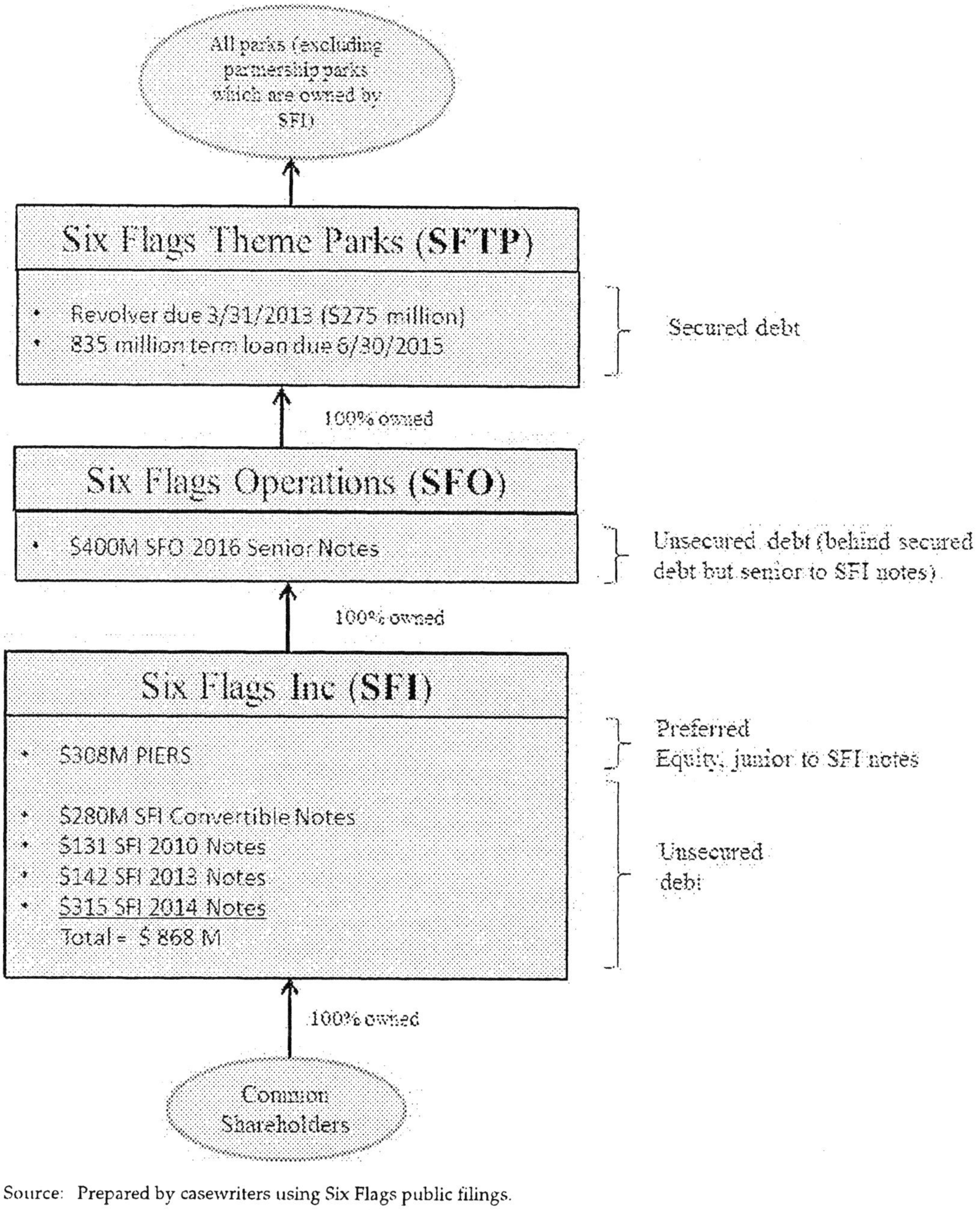

All parks (excluding partnership parks which are owned by SFI)

Six Flags Theme Parks (SFTP)

- Revolver due 3/31/2013 ($275 million)
- $35 million term loan due 6/30/2015

} Secured debt

↑ 100% owned

Six Flags Operations (SFO)

- $400M SFO 2016 Senior Notes

} Unsecured debt (behind secured debt but senior to SFI notes)

↑ 100% owned

Six Flags Inc (SFI)

- $308M PIERS

} Preferred Equity, junior to SFI notes

- $280M SFI Convertible Notes
- $131 SFI 2010 Notes
- $142 SFI 2013 Notes
- $315 SFI 2014 Notes
  Total = $ 868 M

} Unsecured debt

↑ 100% owned

Common Shareholders

Source: Prepared by casewriters using Six Flags public filings.

Notes: As of June 30, 2009, the Company had approximately $2.42 billion of indebtedness outstanding according to public filings, plus $308 of PIERS obligations, including dividends in arrears. SFO senior notes do not include approximately $20 million of accrued interest at the time of the bankruptcy. Six Flags Theme Parks Inc (SFTP) owns directly and indirectly all parks, excluding the Partnership Parks which are owned by SFI. SFI owns interests in Six Flags Over Texas (52%) and Six Flags Over Georgia (29%), including Six Flags White Water Atlanta.

Exhibit 8   Ownership of Six Flags Securities in 2009 (Largest holders)

Bank Debt
JP Morgan
Silverpoint
Beach Point Capital
Davidson Kempner
Sankaty Advisors

SFO Notes
Fidelity
Avenue Capital
H Partners
JP Morgan
Hayman Advisors

SFI Notes
Various hedge funds

Preferred Stock
Resilient Capital Management

Common Equity
RedZone LLC
Cascade Investments
Renaissance Technologies
Och-Ziff Capital
Neuberger Berman

Source: Compiled from SIX Bankruptcy filings & 13-F forms.

Note: Owners are ranked from largest claim to smallest.

Exhibit 9   Six Flags Management and Board of Directors Prior to Bankruptcy

Management Team:

Mark Shapiro, Chief Executive Officer and President [39], since December 2005. From September 2002 to October 2005, Mr. Shapiro served as the Executive Vice President, Programming and Production of ESPN, Inc. From July 2001 to September 2002, he served as Senior Vice President and General Manager, Programming at ESPN.

Jeffrey R. Speed, Executive Vice President and Chief Financial Officer [46], Before joining Six Flags, Mr. Speed served as Senior Vice President and Chief Financial Officer of Euro Disney S.A.S. Prior to Euro Disney, Mr. Speed served as Vice President, Corporate Finance and Assistant Treasurer for The Walt Disney Company.

Mark Quenzel, Executive Vice President Park Strategy and Management [52], oversees all park operations, strategy, and safety for the Six Flags parks. Mr. Quenzel joined Six Flags following 15 years with ESPN, where he served as Senior Vice President, Programming and Production.

Michael Antinoro, Executive Vice President Entertainment and Marketing [44], oversees all aspects of Six Flags' advertising, promotions, entertainment, marketing and communications. Mr. Antinoro formerly served as the Executive Producer of ESPN Original Entertainment (EOE), the core creative group that led the ESPN brand into non-traditional sports and entertainment programming.

Louis Koskovolis, Executive Vice President Corporate Alliances [45], oversees the Corporate Alliances group which focuses on developing key national, regional and local sponsorships for all Six Flags parks and creates cross-promotional platforms which enable Six Flags partners to showcase their products and services while providing Six Flags with added exposure through partners' advertising and marketing assets. Mr. Koskovolis joined Six Flags from his position as Executive Vice President of Multi-Media Sales for ESPN and ABC Sports in addition to serving in leadership roles in the company's National Television Sales and Customer Marketing organizations.

Andrew Schleimer, Executive Vice President of Strategic Development and In-Park Services [31], oversees Six Flags' Strategic Development and In-Park Services, a division that focuses on increasing company revenue and enhancing the park experience through agreements with branded food, beverage, equipment, service and retail partners.

James Coughlin, General Counsel [57], Coughlin served as the Company's General Counsel since 1998. Prior to becoming the Company's chief legal counsel, Mr. Coughlin practiced law at several private law firms, most recently at the former Baer Marks & Upham firm in New York City.

Board of Directors:

Daniel M. Snyder, Chairman of Six Flags, Chairman and owner, Washington Redskins
Mark Shapiro, President of Six Flags
Charles Elliot Andrews, Executive Vice President Sallie Mae
Mark Jennings, Managing Partner, Generation Partners
Jack Kemp, Chairman of Kemp Partners
Robert J. McGuire, Law Offices of Robert J. McGuire
Perry Rogers, President Agassi Enterprises
Dwight Schar, Chairman NVR
Harvey Weinstein, Co-chairman, The Weinstein Company LLC

Source: Six Flags Annual Reports, 2007-2008 and Bloomberg.

Exhibit 10   SFO Bankruptcy Plan

Class	Claim ($MM)	Recovery	Treatment
SFTP *Credit Facility*	1,147	100%	• Paid in full in cash through proceeds of Exit Term Loan and Rights Offering
SFO *Unsecured Bonds, including pre-petition accrued interest*	420	29.7%-45.5%	• To receive approximately 22.9% of the pro forma equity • Subject to dilution by the Long-Term Incentive Plan • Each accepting claimholder shall have the right to participate in the Rights Offering for its limited pro rata share
SFI *Unsecured Bonds*	868	3.0%-4.7%	Right offerings $450 million: • Approximately 69.8% of pro forma equity • Subject to dilution by the Long-Term Incentive Plan • To receive approximately 7.3% of the pro forma equity • Subject to dilution by the Long-Term Incentive Plan
PIERS *Preferred Stock*	308	0%	• No recovery
Common Stock	N/A	0%	• No recovery
Long-term Incentive Plan			• Existing management to receive up to 10% of the pro forma equity, including 3.75% in restricted stock and 3.75% in options.

Source: Six Flags, 2010 8-K filing.

Notes: The range of recovery values depends on the agreed-upon enterprise value, between approximately $1.25 billion and $1.4 billion.

18

Exhibit 11   Historical Financial Data: Six Flags and Cedar Fair (all figures in millions except per-share amounts)

	Six Flags (SIX)							Cedar Fair (FUN)						
	2003	2004	2005	2006	2007	2008	2009	2003	2004	2005	2006	2007	2008	2009
Balance Sheet Data:														
Cash & Equivalents	$433.0	$203.3	$81.5	$24.3	$28.4	$210.3	$164.8	$2.2	$3.4	$4.4	$30.2	$5.5	$13.9	$11.9
Current Assets - Total	433.0	203.3	81.5	24.3	28.4	210.3	164.8	2.2	3.4	4.4	30.2	5.5	13.9	11.9
PP&E, net	2,749.0	2,020.0	1,927.6	1,661.6	1,641.1	1,560.5	1,478.4	777.0	947.0	967.3	1,985.7	1,933.6	1,825.1	1,781.1
Intangibles	1,303.4	1,234.7	1,207.4	1,050.5	1,064.3	1,059.5	1,060.6	-	9.1	10.0	378.9	391.5	276.7	282.2
Total Assets	4,674.7	3,642.2	3,493.1	3,187.6	2,945.3	3,030.8	2,907.7	819.3	993.2	1,024.8	2,510.9	2,418.7	2,186.1	2,145.4
LT Debt due in one-year	326.6	147.5	113.6	114.1	18.7	254.0	308.7	20.0	20.0	20.0	17.5	17.5	17.5	16.0
Total Current Liabilities	512.9	294.5	272.6	291.4	217.3	442.8	539.7	111.7	121.5	130.7	159.3	122.7	115.2	131.5
Long Term Debt	2,359.8	2,125.1	2,128.8	2,126.9	2,239.1	2,044.2	2,097.8	348.6	442.1	450.9	1,759.7	1,735.5	1,706.6	1,610.4
Total Liabilities	3,031.5	2,533.9	2,515.5	2,527.0	2,912.3	3,172.3	3,491.8	510.5	622.7	590.6	2,100.3	2,133.6	2,079.3	2,017.6
Preferred Stock	281.1	282.2	283.4	284.5	285.6	302.4	308.0	-	-	-	-	-	-	-
Common Stock	1,749.7	1,750.4	1,753.3	1,770.2	1,396.0	1,406.8	1,508.6	-	-	-	-	-	-	-
Shareholder's Equity	1,643.2	1,108.3	977.6	660.6	33.0	(141.4)	(584.2)	308.9	370.5	434.2	410.6	285.1	106.8	127.9
Liab. and Shldrs' Equity	4,674.7	3,642.2	3,493.1	3,187.6	2,945.3	3,030.8	2,907.7	819.3	993.2	1,024.8	2,510.9	2,418.7	2,186.1	2,145.4
Operating Data:														
Attendance	N/A	26.8	28.2	24.8	24.9	25.3	23.8	12.2	12.6	12.7	19.3	22.1	22.7	21.1
Ticket revenues	N/A	474.5	524.3	522.7	524.2	534.8	486.0	259.4	276.8	292.4	459.5	552.1	566.3	532.8
In-park revenues	N/A	366.1	398.4	393.8	408.0	427.5	381.9	200.7	211.3	219.1	306.9	360.1	355.9	316.4
Sponsorships/Licensing/Other	N/A	21.0	20.4	25.7	38.6	59.0	42.2	49.9	54.0	57.2	65.0	74.8	74.0	66.9
Total revenues	N/A	861.6	943.2	942.2	970.8	1,021.3	910.1	510.0	542.0	568.7	831.4	987.0	996.2	916.1
COGS	N/A	(71.4)	(82.2)	(80.0)	(81.5)	(86.4)	(77.1)	(52.8)	(56.7)	(57.6)	(80.2)	(92.6)	(90.6)	(84.9)
Cash operating costs	N/A	(524.7)	(567.3)	(623.0)	(661.5)	(627.4)	(625.0)	(281.5)	(312.2)	(318.0)	(441.0)	(554.3)	(550.4)	(514.6)
Cash Flow Data:														
Operating net cash flow	171.7	33.2	121.3	9.8	(37.5)	66.9	77.8	134.9	148.2	160.5	166.4	181.7	215.6	185.2
Capital Expenditures	112.9	107.0	171.2	122.6	115.6	99.2	100.9	39.8	75.9	75.7	59.5	78.5	83.5	15.3
Acquisitions	5.8	-	-	-	54.1	-	-	-	144.3	-	1,253.5	-	(6.4)	-
Investing net cash flow	(362.4)	401.1	(37.1)	(40.0)	64.2	(93.7)	(83.2)	(39.8)	(220.1)	(75.7)	(1,312.9)	(78.5)	(77.1)	(15.3)
Dividends - Preferred	20.8	20.8	20.8	20.8	20.8	5.2	-	(1.1)	(1.7)	(0.7)	24.7	-	-	-
Dividends - Common	-	-	-	-	-	-	-	89.2	93.9	98.8	76.1	102.7	105.1	67.9
Financing net cash flow	262.5	(464.3)	(72.3)	(25.9)	(22.9)	210.5	(40.9)	(95.1)	73.1	(83.8)	1,172.3	(128.3)	(129.4)	(173.3)
Cash interest paid	(186.8)	(197.1)	(181.3)	(190.5)	(199.7)	(163.5)	(87.0)	(24.4)	(24.0)	(26.4)	(90.9)	(138.1)	(120.3)	(117.0)
Cash taxes paid	(3.1)	(3.6)	(4.9)	(4.7)	(5.1)	(7.0)	(4.6)	N/A	(8.8)	(8.8)	(9.7)	(20.7)	(14.6)	(19.0)
Market Value Data:														
Shares Outstanding (millions)	92.6	93.0	93.2	94.4	95.2	97.7	98.3	50.7	53.5	53.8	54.1	54.2	55.1	55.2
Share Price (FYR end)	$7.52	$5.37	$7.71	$5.24	$2.03	$0.31	$0.08	$30.75	$32.90	$28.54	$27.82	$21.13	$12.53	$11.41
Market Cap ($M)	$696.5	$499.6	$718.6	$494.6	$193.3	$30.3	$7.6	$1,558.2	$1,759.5	$1,535.4	$1,504.8	$1,146.3	$690.1	$630.2

Source: Casewriters' compilation from Compustat and company documents.

Exhibit 12   Projections in Management's Proposed Restructuring Plan

(in MM, except per capita numbers)	2009 Proj.	2010 Plan	2011 Plan	2012 Plan	2013 Plan	'09-'13 CAGR
Attendance:	23.8	24.8	25.3	25.3	25.5	1.7%
Per Capita Spending:						
Ticket price	$20.43	$20.43	$20.83	$21.04	$21.26	1.0%
In Park spending	$16.05	$15.98	$16.33	$16.85	$17.10	1.6%
Guest Spending	$36.48	$36.41	$37.16	$37.89	$38.36	1.3%
Total Revenue	$38.25	$38.52	$39.61	$40.66	$41.50	2.1%
P&L Summary:						
Ticket	$486.0	$505.7	$526.9	$532.2	$542.3	2.8%
In Park	381.9	395.6	413.3	426.4	436.0	3.4%
Spons, Int'l, Other Fees	42.2	52.0	62.0	70.0	80.0	17.3%
Total Revenues	$910.2	$953.3	$1,002.2	$1,028.6	$1,058.2	3.8%
Cost of Sales	(77.1)	(81.2)	(83.2)	(85.8)	(87.8)	
Gross Margin	$833.1	$872.1	$919.0	$942.8	$970.5	
Cash Operating Expenses[a]	(619.9)	(619.0)	(638.0)	(634.0)	(639.0)	0.8%
Modified EBITDA	$213.1	$253.1	$281.0	$308.8	$331.5	
Modified EBITDA Margin	23.4%	26.6%	28.0%	30.0%	31.3%	
Other:						
CapEx (Continuing Ops) (Net)	(100.0)	(91.0)	(86.0)	(81.0)	(86.0)	
Int / Divs / Debt Issuance (Net)	(82.9)	(46.8)	(47.7)	(43.9)	(42.0)	
All Other (Cash taxes / Other)	(9.0)	(10.0)	(10.0)	(10.0)	(10.0)	

Source: Six Flags, 2010 8-K. Actual attendance was 25.3 million guests. 2008 per capita spending was $40.30 per visitor, including $21.10 in ticket sales, $16.87 in-park spending, and $2.33 sponsorship/licensing.

[a] Cash Operating expenses were $627.4 million in 2008, and forecast to fall slightly to $619 in 2009 and 2010.

20

138

WORKBRAIN CORP. — A CASE IN EXIT STRATEGY

Teddy Rosenberg wrote this case solely to provide material for class discussion. The author does not intend to illustrate either effective or ineffective handling of a managerial situation. The author may have disguised certain names and other identifying information to protect confidentiality.

Version: (A) 2007-03-13

As Matt Chapman, chief financial officer (CFO) of Workbrain Corp. (Workbrain) sat down to write his memo in the fall of 2003, he knew his words would have enormous impact on the company. Chapman had been asked to consider taking Workbrain public on the Toronto Stock Exchange (TSX). The results were to be presented at the upcoming board of directors meeting. Chapman believed that, in order for his analysis to be meaningful, it had to address a broad array of questions:

- Should Workbrain prepare for an initial public offering (IPO)?
- Was now the right time?
- Which exchange would serve the company better: TSX or NASDAQ?
- Would the shareholders be better off if the company pursued potential acquirers rather than an IPO?
- What other financing alternatives were available?
- Did the company even need to raise money?

WORKBRAIN CORP.

Workbrain Corp. was a Toronto-based company co-founded in November 1999 by its current chief executive officer (CEO), David Ossip. After four years of remarkable growth, the company expected revenues to be more than US$30 million for the year ending 2003.[1] The company had generated $2 million in cash in 2002 and expected to be cash neutral for 2003. As of September 30, 2003, the company had approximately 300 employees. Company headquarters and product development were located in Toronto. The company also maintained a U.S. head office and sales offices in Canada, the United States and Europe.

Workbrain was a leading supplier of workforce management software. The company's products automated a number of labor management tasks:

- Labor forecasting
- Employee scheduling
- Time and attendance monitoring

---

[1] *Like many Canadian companies, Workbrain reported in U.S. dollars because the majority of its revenue came from the United States.*

- Workforce analytics
- Employee self-service applications

These products helped customers with large labor forces to achieve substantial cost savings and improved operational efficiencies:
- Reducing gross payroll costs
- Reducing payroll management costs
- Reducing the use of paper-based forms for time and attendance
- Improving staff utilization through more efficient scheduling
- Improving regulatory compliance
- Identifying and analysing opportunities for additional cost savings through changes to workforce management practices, labor contracts and pay rules.

The company targeted its software to industries characterized by large workforces, complex work rules, multiple sites and inefficient, paper-based workforce management processes. These industries included retailing, manufacturing, financial services, transportation, utilities and the public sectors. Notable customers included:

American Airlines	Avon	Burlington Coat Factory
General Mills	Owens-Illinois	Tennessee Valley Authority
Toronto Police Services	Tyson Foods	Winn-Dixie

The company's software had achieved numerous industry commendations, including being named one of the "Products of the Year" by *HR Executive* magazine and being selected as a "Best of the Web" product by *Forbes* Magazine.

The following example illustrates how one customer used the Workbrain solution:

> In 2001, a large retailer was looking to address the workforce management challenges stemming from its recent acquisition-driven growth. This growth resulted in more than 10,000 employees at several hundred locations across North America. The customer's primary objectives were to standardize payroll practices across the enterprise, reduce payroll errors and abuse, and enable labour cost reporting. This would allow the customer to manage overtime spending. The customer needed a flexible, web-based solution that would operate in a low-bandwidth environment. After implementing the Workbrain software, the customer experienced consistent application of pay rules, increased payroll accuracy, elimination of paper-based processes and a significant reduction in administrative workload. Detailed labour cost information allowed managers to analyse and reduce overtime costs. The customer reported it had reduced gross payroll costs by nearly 3%, a savings of millions of dollars annually.[2]

Workbrain had demonstrated dramatic growth. The company had a three-year compounded annual growth rate (CAGR) in sales projected at 350 per cent for the period 2000 to 2003. Sales were forecast to grow 100 per cent for 2003. Unusual for a technology company, this fast growth had been accompanied by a rapid road to positive cash flow. In its third year of operation, 2002, the company had actually generated $2 million in cash (see Exhibit 1).

---

[2] *Source: Company documents, 2003.*

Workbrain was solving a large problem for large customers. Not surprisingly, these customers paid a great deal for the Workbrain solution with many orders coming in at more than $1 million. These sales were then implemented over a period of several months, with Workbrain recognizing revenue as the implementation proceeded. As a result, the company had excellent visibility into its revenue line for at least two quarters ahead and reasonable insight into the following year's revenue. These large sales, coupled with the fact that Workbrain was a young, private company also meant that prospective customers often had concerns about Workbrain's long-term viability. As a result, Chapman regularly found himself in conversation with clients' CFOs, reassuring them about Workbrain's operational and financial stability. He would share selective financial information with these customers to aid the sales process.

The question of Workbrain's financial stability was a concern to both Chapman and the sales team because the financial questions were asked at a time when Workbrain was most vulnerable — it had won the sales opportunity; its competitors knew it had won the sale; and the competitors also knew that Workbrain would have to review its financial statements and financial viability with prospective customers before closing the deal, giving competitors time to try to reverse the decision.

In April 2003, Workbrain acquired Workforce Logistics Inc., a provider of software solutions, to automate employee scheduling processes in large organizations. With this acquisition, Workbrain enhanced its existing workforce management product line with additional schedule optimization technology. This relatively small acquisition, for a total consideration of $3.8 million,[3] was representative of the sort of selective strategic acquisition the company expected to continue as a way of expanding its product offerings, augmenting its distribution channels and broadening its customer base.

The Industry

Workbrain participated in the market for enterprise-class workforce management software. This software enabled companies to automate the dynamic deployment and management of their workforces, a product area that was distinguished from other well-known categories of business automation software. For example, SAP and Oracle Corp. focused on software commonly called Enterprise Resource Planning (ERP) that automated the management of financial information and customer and supplier relationships. Another well-known category of enterprise software — Human Resource Management (HRM) — in which PeopleSoft had traditionally been the leader, was a back-office solution to manage static human resources information relating to compensation, benefits and personal information.

Although organizations had invested heavily in ERP and HRM systems, considerably less had been invested in Workbrain's category of workforce management systems. One industry analyst estimated that the time and attendance component of the market would alone grow to $400 million in software licenses by 2006. Another industry watcher believed that the combined market for all areas of workforce management, including processes such as employee scheduling and contractor management, greatly exceeded the market for time and attendance solutions alone, and would total $6.8 billion annually in products and services in 2006.

---

[3] The consideration of $3.8 million was made up as follows: cash of $944,000; common shares of 1,115,457 at $2.07 per share; warrants at $0.20 exercisable into 236,495 common shares at an exercise price of $2.07 per share; and acquisition-related costs of $500,000.

The Competition

Growth in the ERP and HRM markets had been slowing, and the major vendors in these categories — SAP, Oracle, PeopleSoft — all multibillion-dollar companies, were making their first forays into the workforce management space. To date, their products provided limited capability but industry watchers expected them to move increasingly into this area through a combination of internal development and acquisitions. Once these companies had their products in place, they would be formidable competitors since they already had a foothold in almost every corporation around the world.

Workbrain also competed directly with a number of companies focused on workforce management. Most significant was Kronos, a NASDAQ-listed company. Although its revenues were considerably larger than Workbrain's, its growth was much slower (see Exhibit 2).

Kronos was founded in 1977, based on electronic time clocks. It evolved to provide a full range of workforce management capabilities. Workbrain was distinguished from Kronos by providing an enterprise-wide solution. Workbrain focused on customers with more than 5,000 employees, and its typical customer had more than 10,000 employees. Workbrain had taken special pains to provide easy integration with ERP and HRM systems — the systems that had been the backbone of corporations. Kronos was more competitive on a department level, servicing 1,200 to 2,500 employees.[4] Additionally, the Workbrain product line was built as an Internet-oriented product from the outset, which made it more modern, flexible and scalable. Nevertheless, Kronos had more than 40,000 customers globally, including a majority of the Fortune 1000 companies.[5]

WORKBRAIN'S FINANCING HISTORY

Workbrain's initial financing came from its founders, who invested US$1 million and held common shares. Workbrain had raised three rounds of venture capital through two classes of preferred shares. The first round, Series A, was completed in April 2000, when just over US$4 million was invested by a group of high-net-worth individuals. The first institutional round came together in December 2000 when Edgestone Capital along with the individual investors put in approximately US$8 million. This investment provided the company with immediate cash, while it pursued U.S. and strategic investors. The company believed investors with these profiles could aid with its U.S. market penetration by lending credibility and marketing heft. In April 2001, Deutsche Bank Alex Brown, a well-regarded Boston-based venture firm associated with a large German Bank, invested US$8 million, and Accenture Technology Ventures, the venture capital arm of the global consulting and systems integration firm, Accenture Inc., invested US$2 million. A complete capitalization table as at September 2003 is shown in Exhibit 3.

WORKBRAIN IN THE FALL OF 2003

Financial statements for the company are provided in Exhibit 4. Chapman had also put together some high-level forecasts for succeeding years (see Exhibit 5). Workbrain had grown remarkably quickly and yet had avoided generating both huge cash losses and huge accounting losses. The company had just over $13.5 million in cash and short-term investments at September 30. The company had a very small (less than $100,000) operating line from a major Canadian bank, but had never drawn on it.

---

[4] *Southwest Securities initiating report on Kronos, September 2004.*
[5] *Kronos website, www.kronos.com, accessed 2006.*

Chapman's projections[6] indicated continuing fast growth for the company albeit at a slightly lower rate: revenues were expected to grow by 100 per cent for 2003 (of which three-quarters had already been completed) and then 69 per cent and 55 per cent in the two subsequent years. Like any fast-growing company, Workbrain always struggled with how much of its revenue growth to re-invest versus how much to let fall to the bottom line. Workbrain generally followed a pattern of keeping income close to a break-even level, while ensuring that cash balances were never at issue. Chapman's projections showed the company continuing to add to its cash balance over the period 2003 to 2005.

Workbrain's venture investors had made their investments in 2000 and 2001. Since venture capitalists (VCs) generally expected to hold their investments for three to five years, Chapman expected the VCs might be starting to think about their exit. Nevertheless, Workbrain's leading VCs, Edgestone and ABS Ventures, both described themselves as patient investors, not looking for an imminent exit. On the other hand, Edgestone expected to be raising its next fund at the beginning of 2004. Workbrain was an early investment for Edgestone and one that it had co-led. To date, the fund had not had any realizations. A successful exit would certainly be helpful in attracting investors to the new fund.

Workbrain's third largest investor was CIBC Capital Partners (CP), who had bought the Accenture Venture Partners portfolio, which included Workbrain. This configuration introduced an interesting quirk: none of the other shareholders knew how much CIBC CP had paid for its position in Workbrain.

From a market perspective, Chapman knew that in high-growth software markets, a race developed to determine the eventual "standard" vendor that would dominate all other players, usually by controlling more than 50 per cent of the market. No leader had yet emerged in the workforce management (WFM) space. Chapman was confident that Workbrain had the strongest product offering but to achieve market dominance, the company had to grow in product breadth, industry coverage and distribution channels. To do so would require investment in salespeople, research and development, and probably the acquisition of companies with complementary products, industry penetration and geographic coverage. Chapman knew that this simultaneous movement on multiple fronts would require a lot of cash.

THE STOCK MARKET

By the fall of 2003, the public stock market seemed to be emerging from what had been one of its worst periods. From the late 1990s to 2001/02, the markets had been on a roller-coaster ride with the dot-com and telecom booms and their subsequent busts. Valuations of public companies were down but seemed to be stabilizing (see Exhibit 6). Through the downward portion of this market ride, very few companies had gone public, and no technology company had gone public in Canada since 2000. Being the first IPO after a long downturn always carried a risk. At the same time, investment bankers with whom Chapman had shared informal conversations indicated that there were signs of latent demand by Canadian institutional investors for technology stocks. Many of these public market investors had defined portions of their portfolios that were required to be invested in Canadian technology stocks, and there were few options to choose from.

---

[6] *Actual projections are not reproduced here. The data provided was produced for this case study specifically. As such, these projections are hypothetical and do not represent the actual projections of Workbrain.*

THE RECOMMENDATION

As Chapman prepared his memo, he knew that one possible recommendation was simply to do nothing. The company had more than $10 million in cash. What was the pressing need for an IPO? More money was always a welcome cushion, but perhaps a better route was to conduct another round of venture financing. The current investors didn't seem to be in any hurry to exit this investment and had even indicated a willingness to invest more money.

Chapman knew that a number of non-financial issues had been preying on management and had set them thinking about an IPO. As a public company, Workbrain would no longer need to enter into long discussions with its customers about its financial viability since that information would be available for all to see. In the same vein, the scrutiny attached to being a public company meant that onlookers tended to see such companies as more disciplined, certainly a boon when trying to close million-dollar sales. But would U.S. or European customers view a TSX-listed company in the same way? After all NASDAQ was the big leagues for technology companies and many Canadian, European and Asian companies had gone the NASDAQ route to prove their mettle.

Chapman's discussions with investment bankers led him to believe that a TSX listing in the near future was viable. For the most part, the TSX was a small-cap market. In addition, the demand/supply imbalance in Canadian technology stocks was attractive, as was the likelihood that a Workbrain IPO would lead to good analyst coverage by the major firms. NASDAQ, although potentially more prestigious, would probably require revenues in the $75 million range for a successful IPO. Chapman had to decide whether to wait to list on the NASDAQ and if so, what, if anything, to do in the interim.

A listing on either the TSX or NASDAQ carried with it the issues faced by any public company: attention from a large number of investors versus simply the handful of venture investors. As a private company, Workbrain spoke directly and in depth to its investors. While both Chapman and his CEO, David Ossip, were accustomed to working with their VCs, neither had been CFO or CEO of a public company. How would they deal with the situation of a large sale slipping into a subsequent quarter, dramatically affecting revenues and earnings for the current reporting period? Because Workbrain was a private company, Ossip and Chapman could sit down with their investors, who were also board members and who had in-depth knowledge of the company, and they could explain the circumstances. As a public company, would the investors be as knowledgeable and open to explanation?

Finally, Chapman knew there was always the possibility of pursuing a sale of the company rather than continuing to go it alone. At a time of a few behemoth software companies, such as SAP, Oracle and PeopleSoft, this option might be the right strategic move.

In deciding on any of these alternatives, Chapman had to consider Workbrain's valuation; he had put together a table of comparable companies (see Exhibit 7).

With time growing short, Chapman had to make a call, and so he started to write his memo.

Exhibit 1

WORKBRAIN CORP. ANNUAL REVENUE, 2000–2003

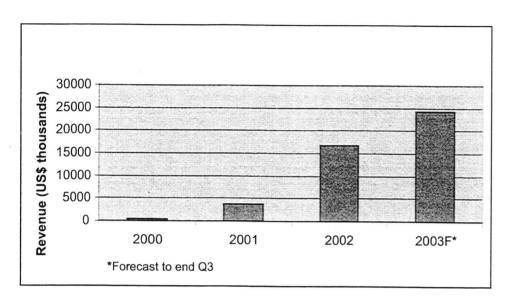

*Forecast to end Q3

Source: Company documents, 2003.

Exhibit 2

WORKBRAIN AND KRONOS — COMPARATIVE REVENUE GROWTH
(IN US$ MILLIONS)

	2001	2002	% Growth
Workbrain	$3.7	$16.8	350%
Kronos	$295.3	$342.4	16%

Sources: Workbrain: Company documents 2003; Kronos: SEC filings 2001 and 2002.

Exhibit 3

CAPITALIZATION TABLE AT SEPTEMBER 30, 2003

	Common		Series A		Series B		Total	% Ownership Outstanding	% Ownership Fully Diluted
	# Shares	Amount Invested	# Shares	Amount Invested	# Shares	Amount Invested			
CEO[1]	12,048,000	1,000,000					12,048,000	36%	31%
Other Founders/Employees	3,884,919						3,884,919	12%	10%
Individual Investors	624,300		2,994,684	3,692,354	2,017,364	3,272,164	5,012,048	15%	13%
Edgestone[2]			249,516	307,653	4,101,434	6,652,526	4,975,250	15%	13%
ABS					4,968,944	8,059,627	4,968,944	15%	13%
Accenture/CIBCCP					1,242,236	2,014,907	1,242,236	4%	3%
Workforce Logistics[3]	1,115,457	2,308,996					1,115,457	3%	3%
Total Outstanding	17,672,676		3,244,200		12,329,978		33,246,854	100%	
ESOP	4,944,841						4,944,841		13%
Warrants[4]									
Edgestone[5]	655,129						655,129		2%
WFL	236,495	47,299					236,495		1%
Fully Diluted	23,509,141		3,244,200		12,329,978		39,083,319		100%

Notes:

All amounts are in U.S. dollars. The exchange rate at September 2003 was approximately US$1 = CDN$1.35.

[1] *Shares are held by the CEO's family trust and holding company.*

[2] *Edgestone acquired common shares and Series A preferred shares from various employees and high net worth individuals.*

[3] *Workbrain acquired Workforce Logistics on April 1, 2003.*

[4] *Warrant Exercise Prices WFL:$2.07 ATV: $1.61.*

[5] *Edgestone acquired these warrants from ATV, which had received them as part of a strategic sales agreement.*

146

Exhibit 4

WORKBRAIN BALANCE SHEET
(in US$ thousands)

	September 30,	December 31,	
	2003	2002	2001
Assets			
Current Assets			
Cash and Equivalents	$5,186	$6,370	$5,114
Short-term Investments	8,427	8,931	8,376
Accounts Receivable	6,905	5,027	1,562
Other	2,661	2,380	893
Total Current Assets	23,179	22,708	15,945
Property and Equipment	1,992	1,315	808
Intangibles	727		
Goodwill	2,711		
Total Assets	$28,609	$24,023	$16,753
Liabilities & Shareholders' Equity			
Current Liabilities			
Accounts Payable	$515	$777	$333
Accrued Payroll	2,182	1,549	670
Accrued Liabilities	1,301	983	37
Deferred Revenue	9,934	10,390	2,649
Capital Lease - Current	48		
Leasehold Inducements - Current	48	41	41
Total Current Liabilities	14,028	13,740	3,730
Long-term Liabilities			
Capital Lease – Net of Current	65		
Leasehold Inducements - Net of Current	80	99	139
Total Long-Term Liabilities	145	99	139
Total Liabilities	14,173	13,839	3,869
Shareholders' Equity			
Common Shares	3,729	1,007	1,000
Class A Preferred Shares	4,680	4,680	4,680
Class B Preferred Shares	19,963	19,963	19,963
Contributed Surplus	1,806	1,756	1,523
Deferred Stock-based Compensation	(72)	(128)	(270)
Cumulative Translation Adjustment	(127)	(127)	(127)
Deficit	(15,543)	(16,967)	(13,885)
Total Shareholders' Equity	14,436	10,184	12,884
Total Liabilities & Shareholders' Equity	$28,609	$24,023	$16,753

147

Exhibit 4 (continued)

INCOME STATEMENT
(in US$ thousands)

	Nine Months Ended September 30,		Year Ended December 31,		
	2003	**2002**	**2002**	**2001**	**2000**
Revenue					
Licence	$7,840	$2,839	$4,320	$1,181	$164
Service, Maintenance	16,481	8,434	12,529	2,557	253
Net Revenue	24,321	11,273	16,849	3,738	417
Cost of Revenue					
Licence	279	9	83		
Service, Maintenance	11,595	5,129	8,264	2,142	344
Total Cost of Revenue	11,874	5,138	8,347	2,142	344
Gross Profit	12,447	6,135	8,502	1,596	73
Operating Expenses					
Sales and Marketing	6,216	3,958	5,905	4,989	989
Research and Development	3,442	2,247	3,456	3,366	1,628
General and Administration	1,321	1,433	2,215	1,783	1,182
Amortization of Intangibles	211				
Amortization of Stock-based Comp.	3	259	268	711	445
Total Operating Expenses	11,193	7,897	11,844	10,849	4,244
Income (Loss) from Operations	1,254	(1,762)	(3,342)	(9,253)	(4,171)
Interest Income (net)	170	204	260	476	124
Accretion on Preferred Shares				(529)	(458)
Net Income (Loss)	1,424	(1,558)	(3,082)	(9,306)	(4,505)

Exhibit 4 (continued)

CONSOLIDATED STATEMENTS OF CASH FLOWS
(in US$ thousands)

	Nine Months Ended September 30,		Year Ended December 31,		
	2003	2002	2002	2001	2000
Cash flows from operating activities					
Net Income (Loss)	$1,424	($1,558)	($3,082)	($9,306)	($4,505)
Adjustments to reconcile net income (loss) to net cash					
provided by (used by) operating activities					
Depreciation	1,153	427	606	386	111
Amortization of intangibles	211				
Amortization of stock-based comp	59	355	375	751	445
Amortization of leasehold inducements	(12)	(30)	(40)	(36)	
Accretion on preferred shares				529	458
Loss on disposal of fixed assets				32	
Change in operating assets and liabilities					
Accounts Receivable	(1,517)	(2,860)	(3,465)	(1,141)	(422)
Other Assets	(202)	(1,327)	(1,487)	(570)	(298)
Accounts Payable	(41)	693	444	(135)	456
Accrued Payroll	628	1,054	879	556	114
Accrued Liabilities	(211)	929	946	(115)	152
Deferred revenue	(554)	596	7,741	2,160	489
Net cash provided by (used for) operating activities	938	(1,721)	2,917	(6,889)	(3,000)
Cash flows from investing activities					
Purchase of short-term investments	(8,427)	(8,931)	(8,931)	(8,870)	
Sale of short-term investments	8,931	8,376	8,376	494	
Payments made on the acquisition of the net operating assets					
of Workforce Logistics Inc., net of cash required	(1,390)				
Purchase of property and equipment	(1,602)	(884)	(1,113)	(433)	(641)
Net cash used for investing activities	(2,488)	(1,439)	(1,668)	(8,809)	(641)
Cash flows from financing activities					
Repayment of obligations under capital lease	(47)				
Proceeds from issuance of common shares upon exercise of					
stock options	413		7		
Proceeds from issuance of Class A preferred shares					4,055
Proceeds from issuance of Class B preferred shares				11,750	7,773
Receipt of payment from share purchase loans receivable				108	847
Net cash provided by financing activities	366		7	11,858	12,675
Effect of exchange rate on cash					(127)
Change in cash and cash equivalents	(1,184)	(3,160)	1,256	(3,840)	9,034
Cash and cash equivalents, beginning of period	6,370	5,114	5,114	8,954	47
Cash and cash equivalents, end of period	$5,186	$1,954	$6,370	$5,114	$9,081

Source: Company files.

Exhibit 5

KEY FINANCIAL DATA — FORECASTS
(in US$ thousands)

| | Years Ending December 31 | | |
	2003	2004	2005
Revenue			
Licence	$10,350	$16,350	$23,000
Service, Maintenance	23,450	40,650	65,500
Net Revenue	33,800	57,000	88,500
Growth Percentage	101%	69%	55%
Cost of Revenue			
Licence	325	300	675
Service, Maintenance	16,500	28,050	47,650
Total Cost of Revenue	16,825	28,350	48,325
Gross Profit	16,975	28,650	40,175
Operating Expenses			
Sales and Marketing	8,800	13,000	17,000
Research and Development	5,150	8,600	13,250
General and Administration	1,625	4,500	7,100
Amortization of Intangibles	350	365	200
Amortization of Stock-based Compensation	85	1,250	1,000
Total Operating Expenses	16,010	27,715	38,550
Income (Loss) from Operations	965	935	1,625
Interest Income (Net)	(230)	475	1,250
Net Income (Loss)	735	1,410	2,875
Cash and Equivalents, Including Short-term Investments	14,500	18,000	23,000
Working Capital	9,000	13,500	18,500

Source: Data created by author.

Exhibit 6

PRICE TO LAST QUARTER ANNUALIZED REVENUE MULTIPLES

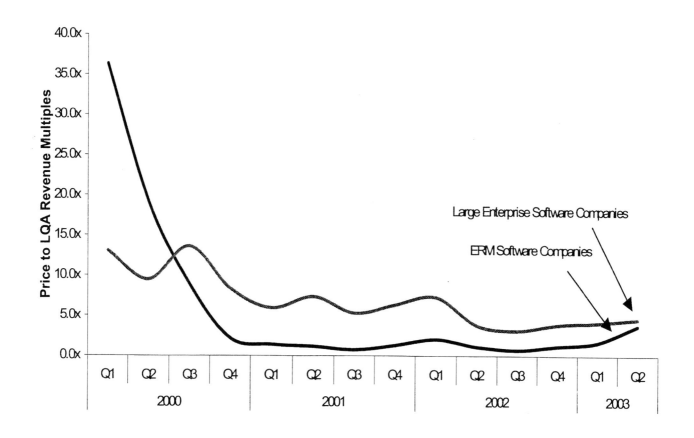

Source: Compiled from publicly available data, 2003.

Exhibit 7

COMPARABLE COMPANY ANALYSIS

	Market Cap	TEV	TEV/Revenue			TEV/EBITDA		P/E		Revenue Growth
			LTM	CY2003e	CY2004e	CY2003e	CY2004e	CY2003e	CY2004e	CY02–04e
Vendors with ERM Capability										
Oracle	65,160	58,969	6.2×	6.1×	5.8×	15.2×	14.2×	27.8×	26.4×	8.0%
SAP	34,969	33,005	4.4×	4.3×	4.1×	25.1×	13.8×	28.9×	27.0×	14.0%
PeopleSoft	6,269	4,292	2.2×	2.2×	2.1×	12.5×	11.8×	30.8×	31.3×	6.7%
Siebel	4,876	2,874	2.0×	2.1×	2.0×	14.2×	9.7×	78.3×	36.4×	(12.8)%
Lawson Software	704	445	1.3×	1.3×	1.2×	n/a	n/a	128.3×	82.9×	(10.3)%
Average			**3.2×**	**3.2×**	**3.0×**	**16.7×**	**8.8×**	**57.8×**	**40.8×**	
ERM Companies										
Kronos	1131	1028	2.7×	2.6×	2.3×	15.0x	n/a	32.2×	neg	26.2%
Concur Technologies	351	333	6.0×	6.6×	4.5×	47.0×	n/a	111.4×	neg	60.4%
Ultimate Software	145	139	2.3×	2.3×	2.0×	n/a	n/a	neg	neg	28.3%
Niku Corp,	75	56	1.3×	n/a	n/a	n/a	n/a	neg	neg	n/a
Saba Software	51	4	0.0×	0.7×	0.5×	nmf	n/a	neg	15.2×	0.4%
Docent	51	15	0.5×	0.5×	n/a	n/a	n/a	neg	neg	n/a
Average			**2.1×**	**2.5×**	**2.3**	**31.0×**	**n/a**	**71.8×**	**15.2×**	
Canadian Software										
Cognos Inc.	3,161	2,876	4.7×	4.5×	3.9×	n/a	n/a	37.4×	31.9×	22.5% *
Open Text Corp.	810	694	3.8×	3.6×	2.8×	n/a	n/a	26.7×	25.3×	17.3.%*
High-Growth Software										
Altiris Inc.	746	596	6.8×	6.1×	4.5×			59.7×	40.9×	58.8%*
Netscreen Technologies	2110	1769	7.2×	6.5×	4.4×			41.4×	38.8×	74.4%*
Websense Inc.	558	391	5.1×	4.8×	3.9×			33.2×	28.2×	31.2%*
Average			**5.8×**	**5.8×**	**4.3×**			**44.8×**	**36.0×**	

*Most recent year only

Source: Compiled from publicly available data, 2003.